AUTHENTIC TRANSCRIPTIONS
WITH NOTES AND TABLATURE

BEST OF '90s ROCK

ISBN 0-7935-9729-3

7777 W. Bluemound Rd. P.O. Box 13819 Milwaukee, WI 53213

Visit Hal Leonard Online at
www.halleonard.com

BEST OF '90s ROCK

INTRODUCTION - THE DIVERSITY OF '90S ROCK

This past decade of rock music has seen just about every aspect of the genre explored, from the huge resurgence of ska to folk music to swing to punk rock. The cold, technical sound of '80s electronica combined with the big-guitar metal sounds of the same decade created an entirely new sound–throw in some hip hop, you've got Rage Against the Machine; throw in a little blues, you've got Kenny Wayne Shepherd.

Surprises of the '90s included the re-emergence of guitar legend Eric Clapton, whose album Unplugged *contained brand-new tracks as well as the beautiful acoustic reworking of his classic, "Layla." It was this album that played a major role in many electric bands suddenly going acoustic, as well as inspiring the MTV "Unplugged" series. The '90s also saw the return of the wordsmith in rock. Beck's first big hit, "Loser," was praised by Beat veteran Alan Ginsberg as being one of the best poems of the decade, while Nirvana's "Nevermind" was hailed by critics and listeners alike as an anthem for the times. On the female front, folk songstress Tracy Chapman took her stories of inner city life and conflicts to new heights, while Alanis Morissette put her Sylvia Plath ideology to music, paving the way for a whole new generation of angry, disaffected women in rock. The efforts of both women revitalized the music community by helping bring about the first annual conference of women's music: Lilith Fair.*

The rapid-fire creation of new musical styles left music connoisseurs scrabbling to come up with names for all the new genres. The Mighty Mighty Bosstones still get labeled as ska - mostly because they have a horn section - but they lean more towards heavy guitar rock than classic mod. Nirvana and Soundgarden were both considered "grunge" when the bands came out, even though they sounded nothing like each other and really shared no characteristics past being from Seattle. Punk rock took on measurable market value again when the Offspring began getting radio play, much to the astonishment of adults who had grown up listening to the Sex Pistols and had long since decided that punk was dead.

This all leads, of course, to speculation of what the next ten years will bring to rock. Even now, the traditionally heavy-metal Ozzfest has been infiltrated by the strains of Latin and Armenian music with the emergence of groups like Puya and System of a Down. Trade schools based entirely around the music industry continue to spring up and continue to have high enrollment rates, while more and more venues for live music have opened all over the country. With the recent explosion of home recording studios and independent labels, cheap production costs for high-quality releases, and the hundreds of distribution companies worldwide that are more than willing to handle even the tiniest projects, the field is wide open for just about anything to happen.

- Holly Day

Black Hole Sun

Words and Music by Chris Cornell

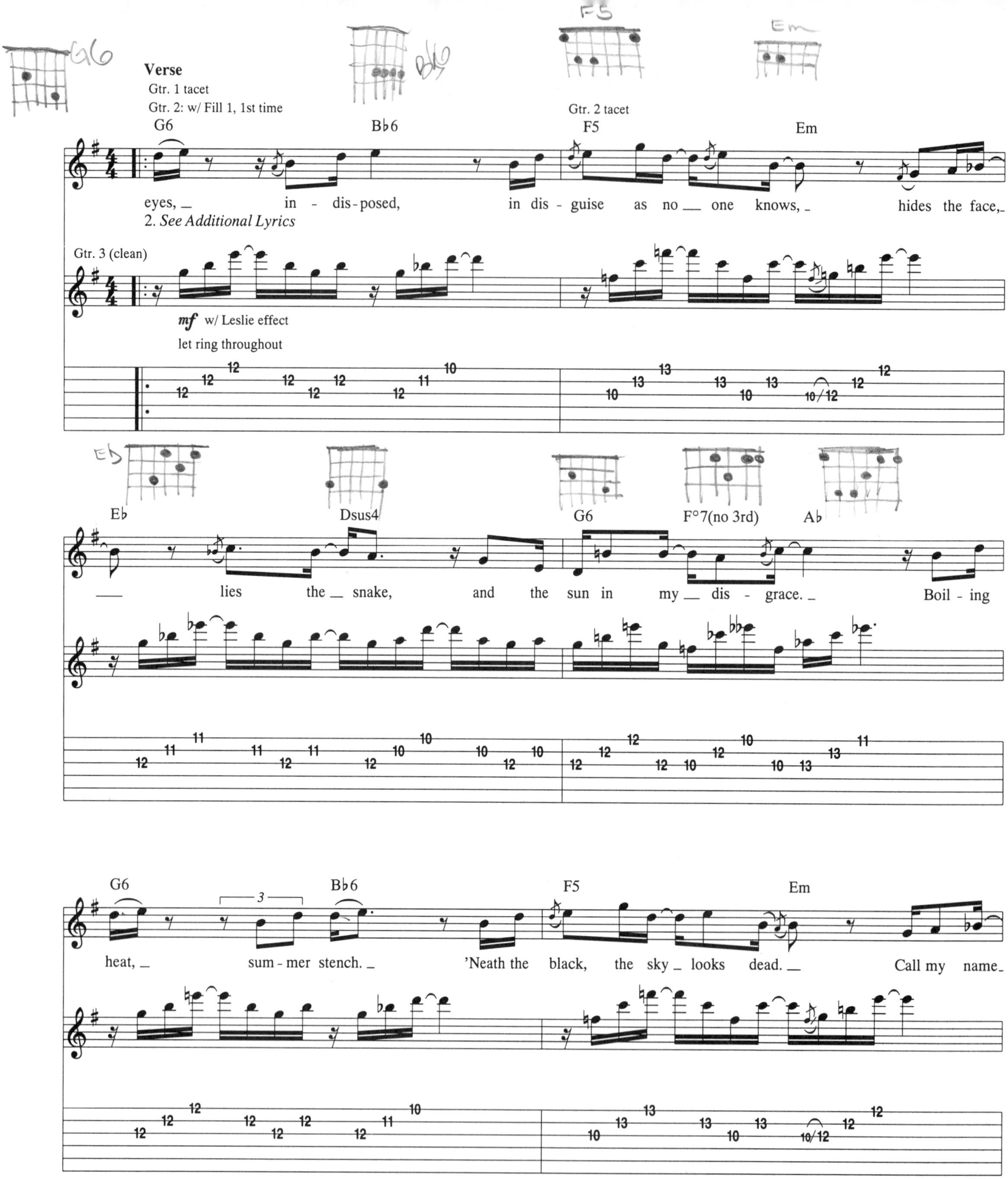

Verse

Gtr. 1 tacet
Gtr. 2: w/ Fill 1, 1st time

G6 Bb6 Gtr. 2 tacet F5 Em

eyes, _ in - dis - posed, in dis - guise as no _ one knows, _ hides the face, _

2. *See Additional Lyrics*

Gtr. 3 (clean)

mf w/ Leslie effect
let ring throughout

Eb Dsus4 G6 F°7(no 3rd) Ab

_ lies the _ snake, and the sun in my _ dis - grace. _ Boil - ing

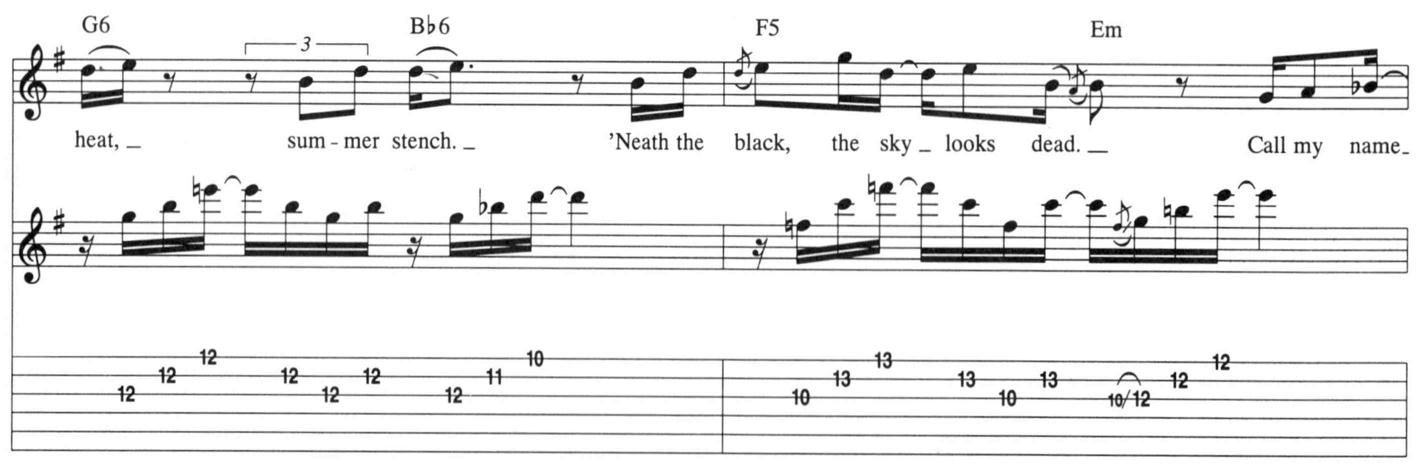

G6
Bb6
F5
Em
3
heat, _ sum - mer stench. _ 'Neath the black, the sky _ looks dead. _ Call my name _

Fill 1
Gtr. 2
(19)
(19)

E♭
Dsus4
G6
F°7(no 3rd)
A♭
through the cream and I'll hear you scream a - gain.
Black hole
Chorus
Gtr. 3 tacet
D♭sus4
D7(no 3rd)
G5
G5/F
B♭
sun, won't you come and wash a - way the rain?
Black hole
Gtr. 1
w/ dist.
E♭sus4
D7(no 3rd)
1.
C
D
sun, won't you come? Won't you come? Won't you come?
2. Stut - ter -
2.
C
B♭
E♭sus4
D7(no 3rd)
Black hole
sun, won't you come and

G5 G5/F B♭ E♭sus4 D7(no 3rd)
wash a - way the rain? Black hole sun, won't you come? Won't you come?
w/ Voc. Fig. 1, 4 times
C B♭ D C B♭ D
To Coda
Won't you come? Oh, won't you come?
Rhy. Fig. 1
End Rhy. Fig. 1
Gtr 1: w/ Rhy. Fig. 1, simile
C B♭ D C B♭ D
Won't you come?
Guitar Solo
Gtr. 1: w/ Rhy. Fig. 2, 6 times
N.C. F6 sus♯4 sus2 N.C. F6 sus♯4 sus2
*Gtr. 4 (dist.)
f ** w/ wah-wah
full
full
*Two gtrs. arr. for one.
** + = closed (treble), ° = open (bass).
Voc. Fig. 1
Black hole sun. Black hole sun.
Rhy. Fig. 2
Gtr. 1

N.C.
F6 sus♯4 sus2
full
full
N.C.
F6 sus♯4 sus2
N.C
F6 sus♯4 sus2
1/2
full
full
full
1/2
N.C.
F6 sus♯4 sus2
1/2
1/2
Verse
Gtrs. 1 & 4 tacet
F5
G5
G6
B♭6
Gtr. 1
3. Hang my head, drown my fear, till you
Gtr. 3
F
Em
D.S. al Coda
(take 2nd ending)
all just dis - ap - pear.
Black hole
Gtr. 3
Gtr. 1
divisi

*Let echo fade out on multi repeat setting.

Additional Lyrics

2. Stuttering, cold and damp.
Steal the warm wind, tired friend.
Times are gone for honest men,
And sometimes far too long for snakes.
In my shoes, a walking sleep.
In my youth I pray to keep.
Heaven send hell away.
No one sings like you anymore.

Blue on Black

Words and Music by Kenny Wayne Shepherd, Tia Sillers and Mark Selby

Chorus
Gtr. 1: w/ Rhy. Fig. 1, 2 times, simile
Gtr. 4: w/ Fill 1, 3rd time
D5 Csus2 D5 Csus2 D5 N. C. Cadd9 G/B G
blue on black, tears on a riv - er, push on a shove, it don't mean much.
* Gtr. 3
(elec.)
Riff A1
End Riff A1
mf
w/ dist & tremolo effect
P.M.
let ring
1/4
* Two gtrs. arr. for one.
Gtr. 3: w/ Riff A1
D5 Csus2 D5 Csus2 D5 N. C. Cadd9 G/B G
Jok - er on Jack, match on a fire, cold on ice, a dead man's touch.
D5 N. C. Cadd9 G/B G
Whis - per on a scream does - n't change a thing, 1., 3. don't 2., 4. does - n't bring you
Gtr. 1
1/4
Gtr. 3
P.M.
let ring
1/4
Fill 1
Gtr. 4
T
A
B

To Coda 1
To Coda 2
To Coda 3
A5
G
back.
Blue on
Gtr. 1: w/ Rhy. Fig. 1, 2 times, simile
Gtr. 3: w/ Riff A1, 2 times, simile
D5 Csus2 D5 Csus2 D5 N. C. Cadd9 G/B G
black.
Oh, yeah.
Blue on
Gtr. 4 (elec.)
w/ dist. & *harmonizer
1/4
full
* Set to harmonize one octave above.
D5 Csus2 D5 Csus2 D5 N. C. Cadd9 G/B G
black.
P.M.
full

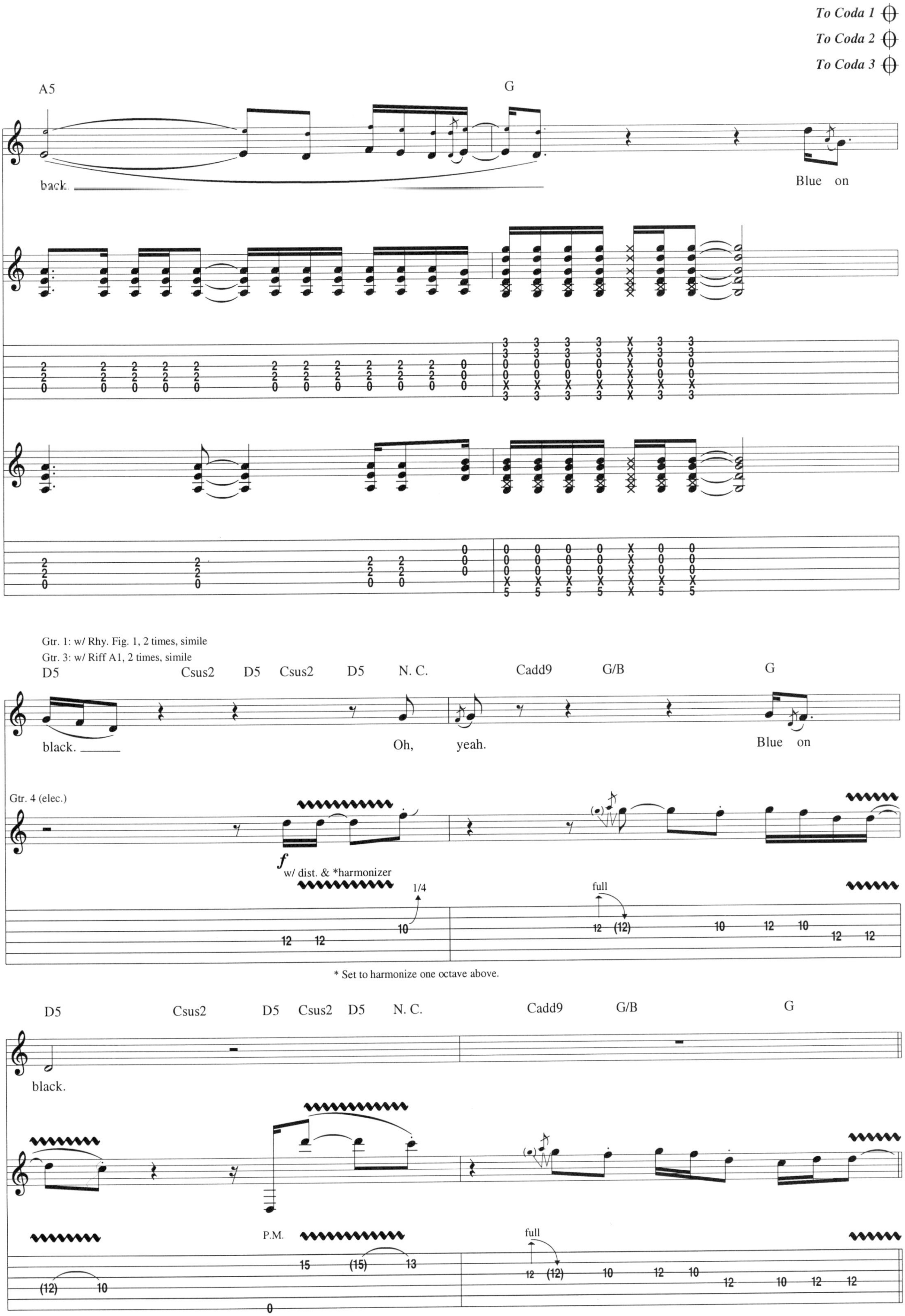

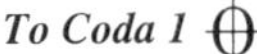

Verse
Gtr. 1: w/ Rhy. Fig. 1, 8 times, simile
Gtr. 3: w/ Riff A1, 8 times, simile
D5 Csus2 D5 Csus2 D5 N. C. Cadd9 G/B G D5 Csus2 D5 Csus2 D5 N. C. Cadd9 G/B G
2. Blind, oh, now I see.
P.M.
harmonizer off
P.M.
D5 Csus2 D5 Csus2 D5 N. C. Cadd9 G/B G D5 Csus2 D5 Csus2 D5 N. C.
Truth, lies, and in be - tween.
P.M.
P.M.
Cadd9 G/B G D5 Csus2 D5 Csus2 D5 N. C. Cadd9 G/B G
Wrong can't be un -
P.M.
P.M.
D5 Csus2 D5 Csus2 D5 N. C. Cadd9 G/B G D5 Csus2 D5 Csus2 D5 N. C.
done. Oh, slipped
P.M.
P.M.

D.S. al Coda 1

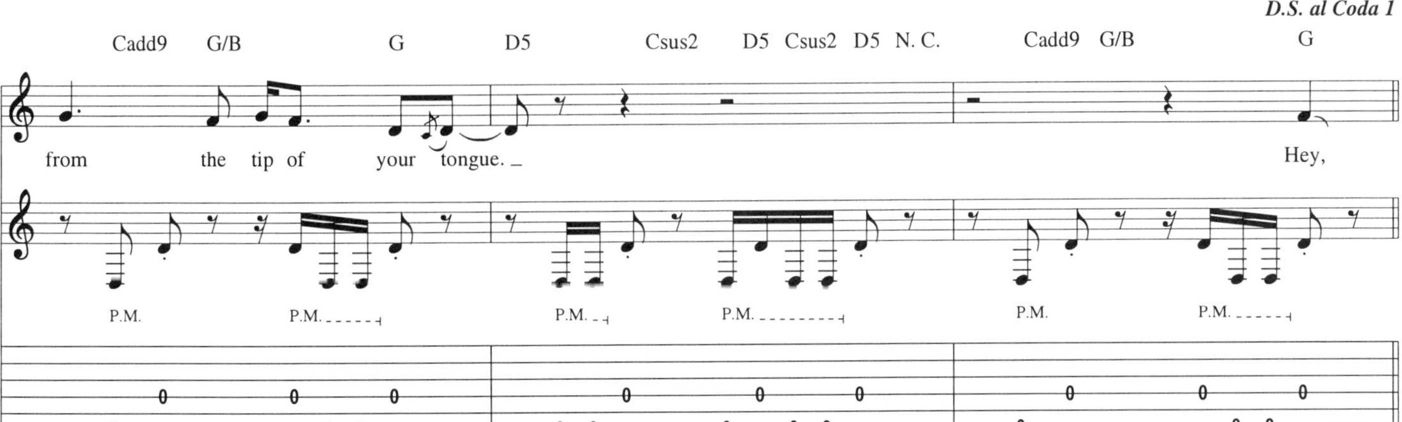

Coda 1

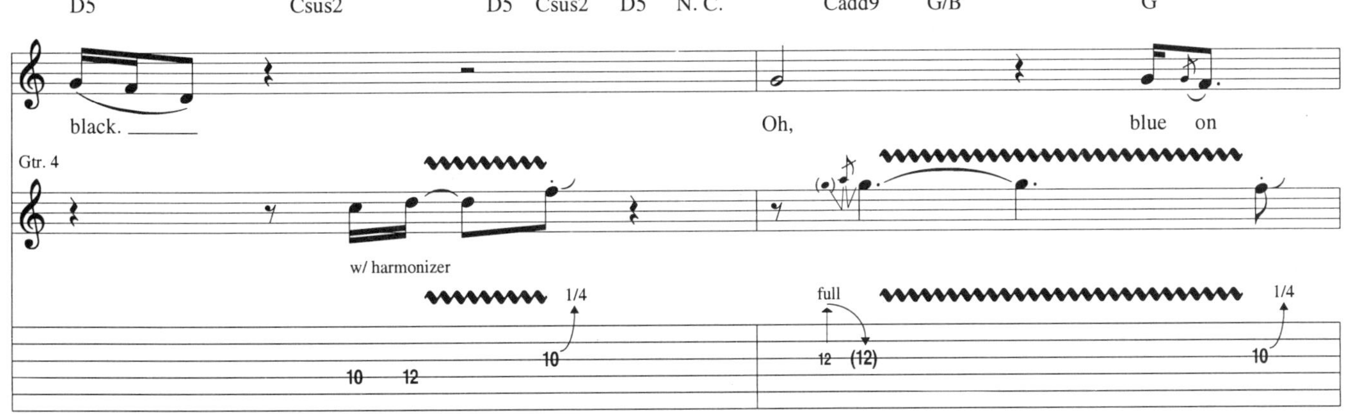

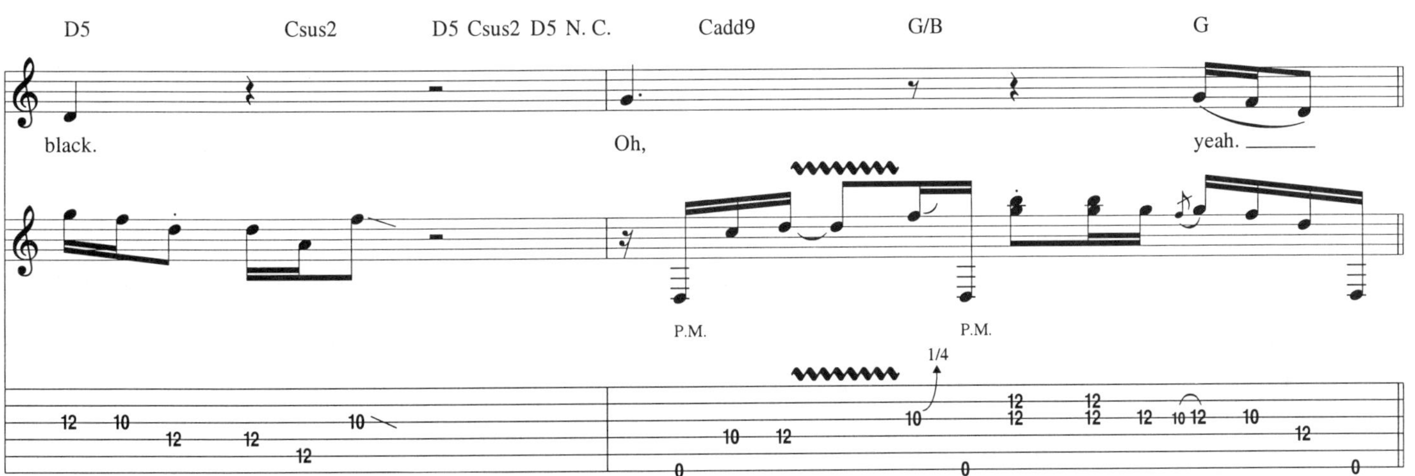

Guitar Solo

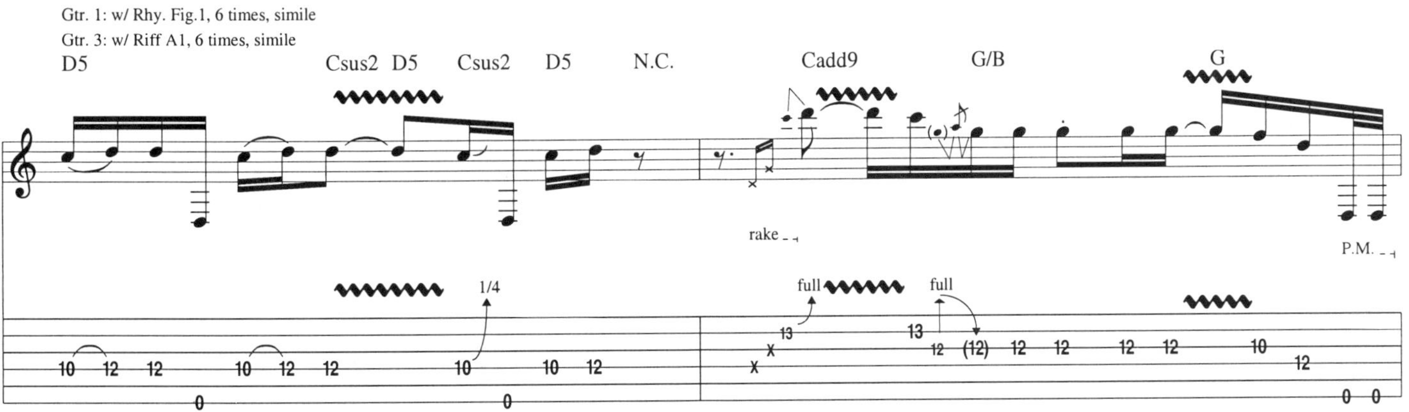

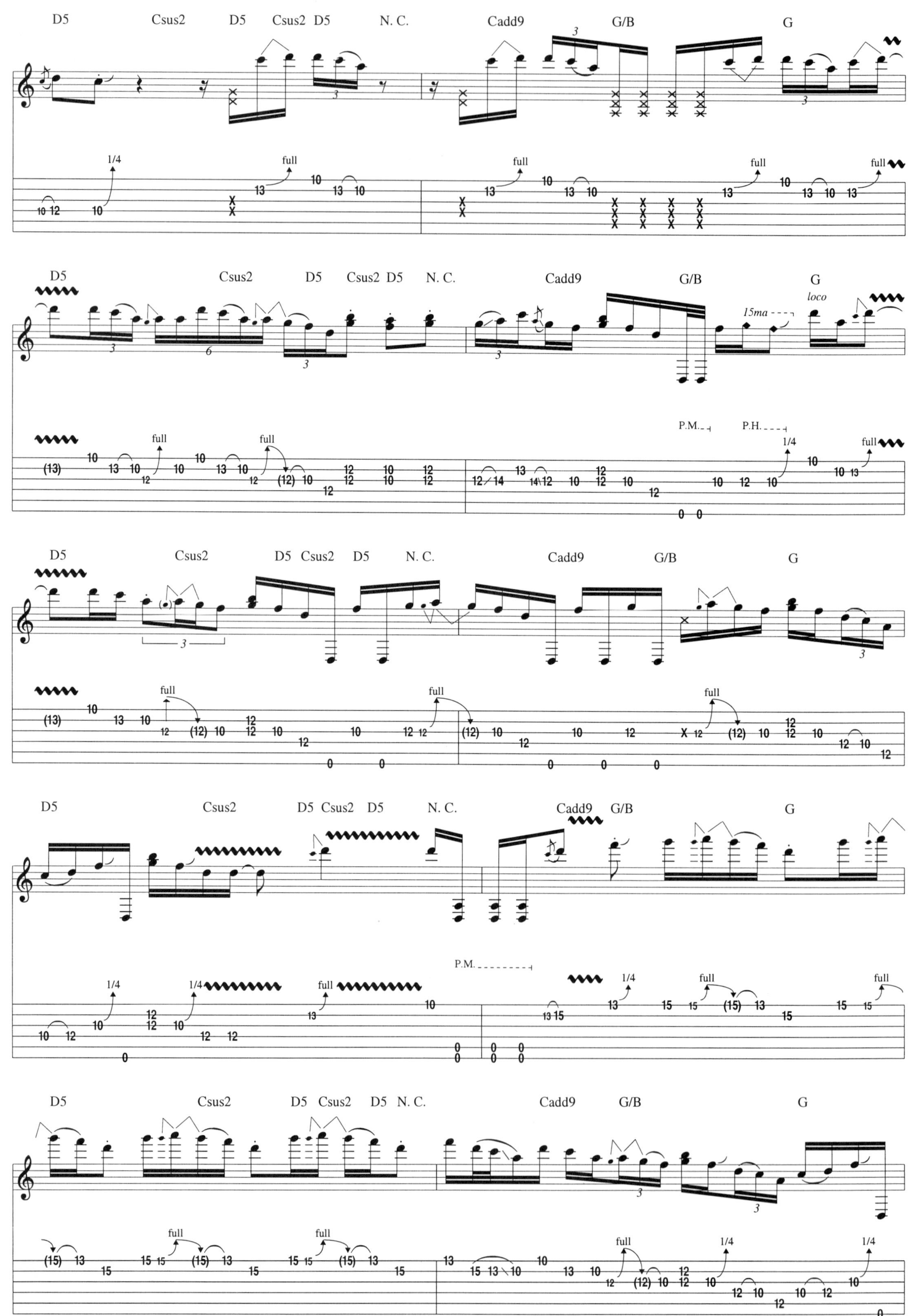
D5 Csus2 D5 Csus2 D5 N. C. Cadd9 G/B G
D5 Csus2 D5 Csus2 D5 N. C. Cadd9 G/B G
15ma
loco
P.M.
P.H.
D5 Csus2 D5 Csus2 D5 N. C. Cadd9 G/B G
D5 Csus2 D5 Csus2 D5 N. C. Cadd9 G/B G
P.M.
D5 Csus2 D5 Csus2 D5 N. C. Cadd9 G/B G
full
1/4

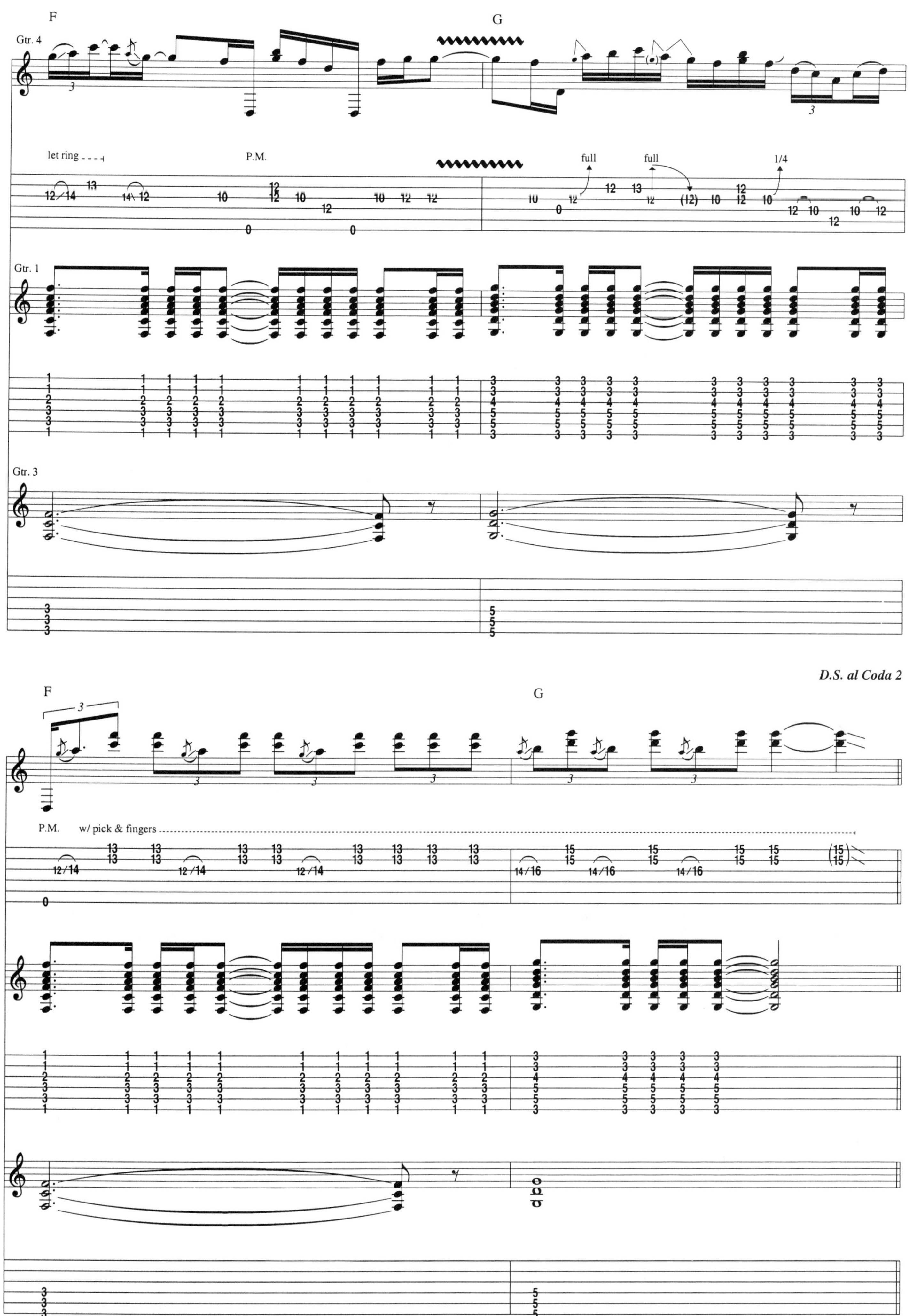

F
G
Gtr. 4
let ring
P.M.
full
full
1/4
Gtr. 1
Gtr. 3
D.S. al Coda 2
F
G
P.M.
w/ pick & fingers

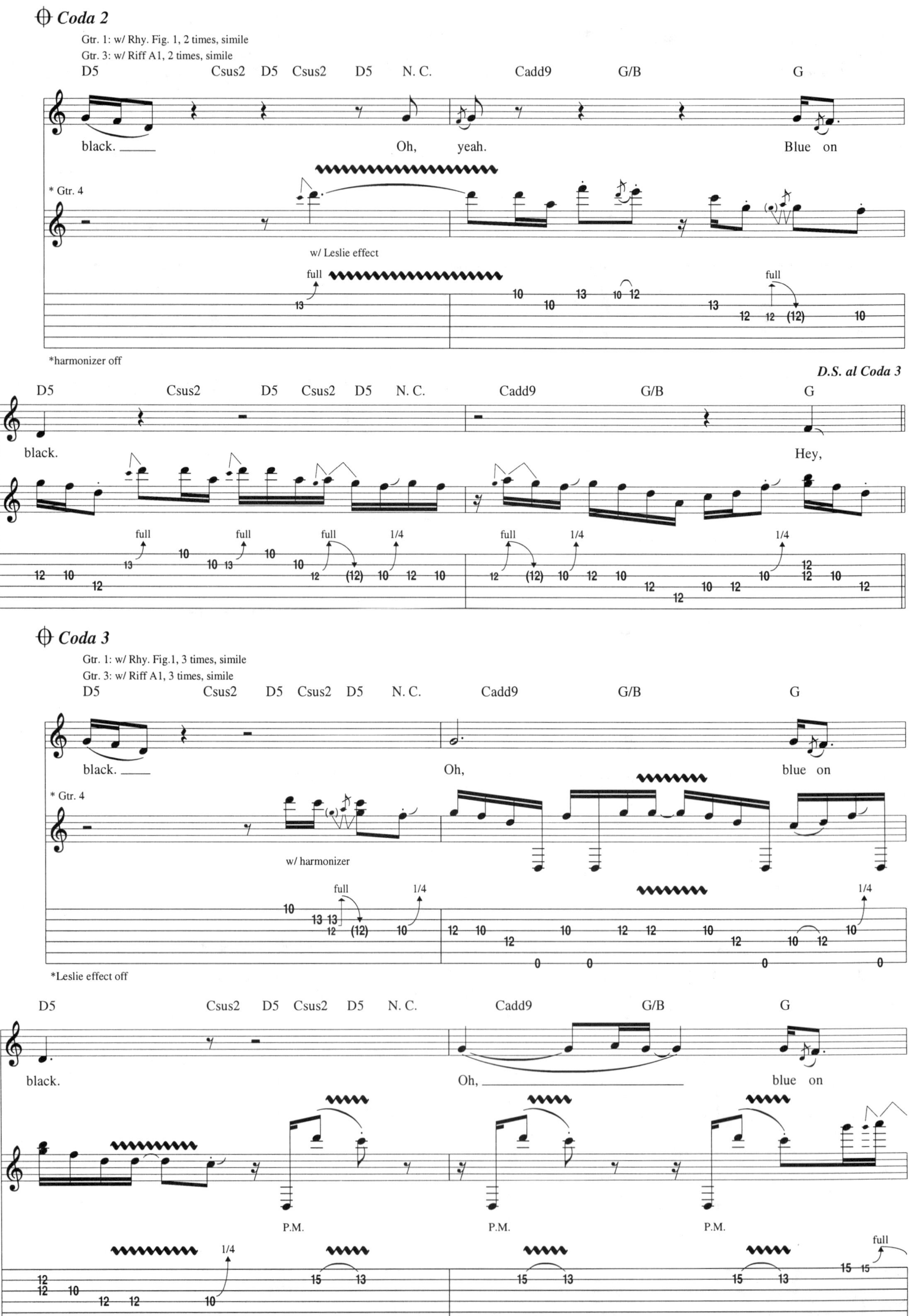
Coda 2
Gtr. 1: w/ Rhy. Fig. 1, 2 times, simile
Gtr. 3: w/ Riff A1, 2 times, simile
D5 Csus2 D5 Csus2 D5 N. C. Cadd9 G/B G
black. Oh, yeah. Blue on
* Gtr. 4
w/ Leslie effect
full
full
*harmonizer off
D.S. al Coda 3
D5 Csus2 D5 Csus2 D5 N. C. Cadd9 G/B G
black. Hey,
full full full 1/4 full 1/4 1/4
Coda 3
Gtr. 1: w/ Rhy. Fig.1, 3 times, simile
Gtr. 3: w/ Riff A1, 3 times, simile
D5 Csus2 D5 Csus2 D5 N. C. Cadd9 G/B G
black. Oh, blue on
* Gtr. 4
w/ harmonizer
full 1/4 1/4
*Leslie effect off
D5 Csus2 D5 Csus2 D5 N. C. Cadd9 G/B G
black. Oh, blue on
P.M. P.M. P.M.
1/4 full

D5 Csus2 D5 Csus2 D5 N. C. Cadd9 G/B G
black. Oh, blue on
full
P.M.
D5 Csus2 D5 Csus2 D5 N. C. Cadd9 G/B
black.
Gtr. 4
P.M.
Gtr. 1
Gtr. 3
let ring

Counting Blue Cars

Words by J. R. Richards

Music by Scot Alexander, George Pendergast, Rodney Browning, J. R. Richards and Gregory Kolanek

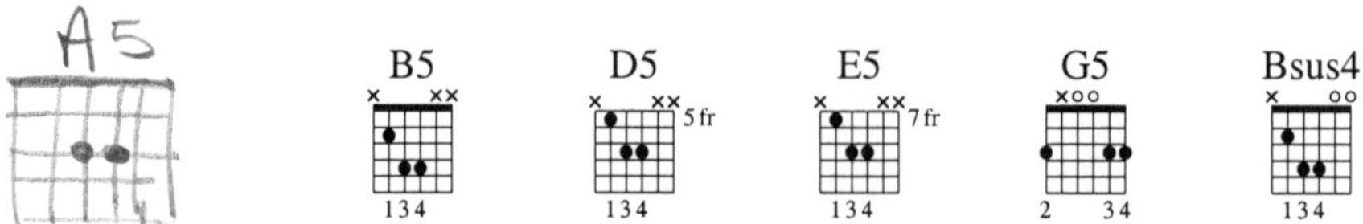

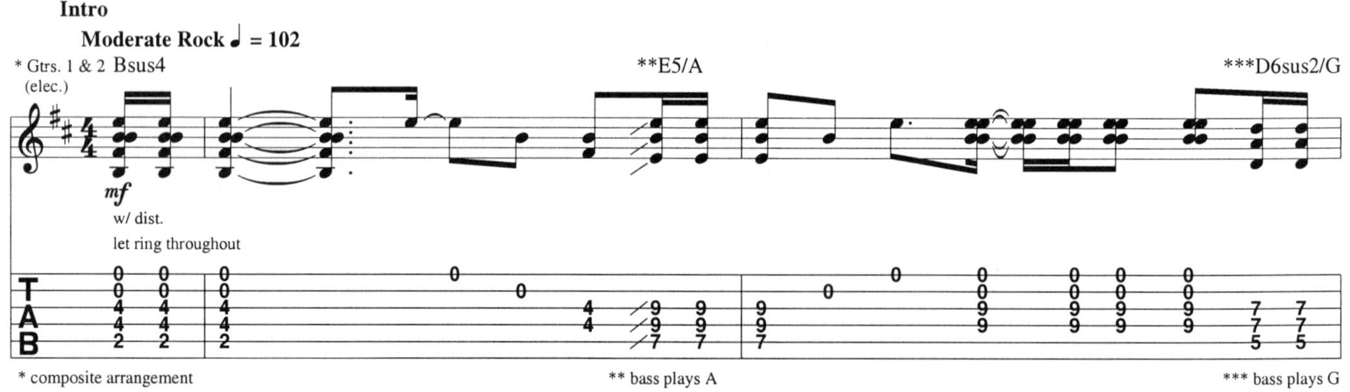

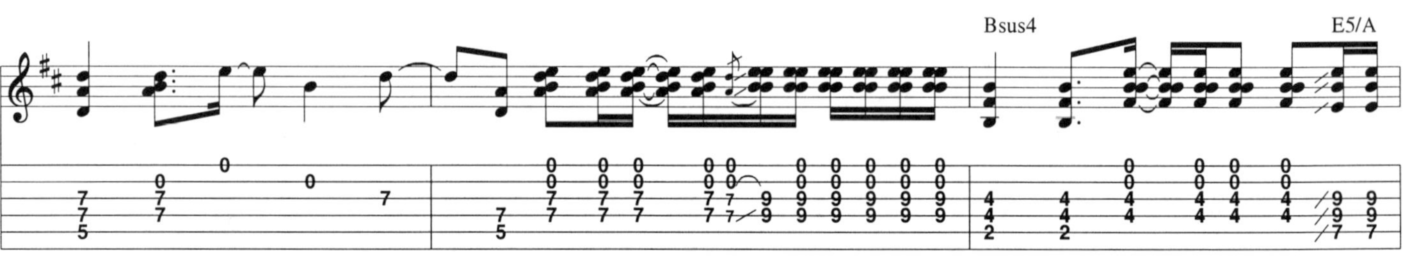

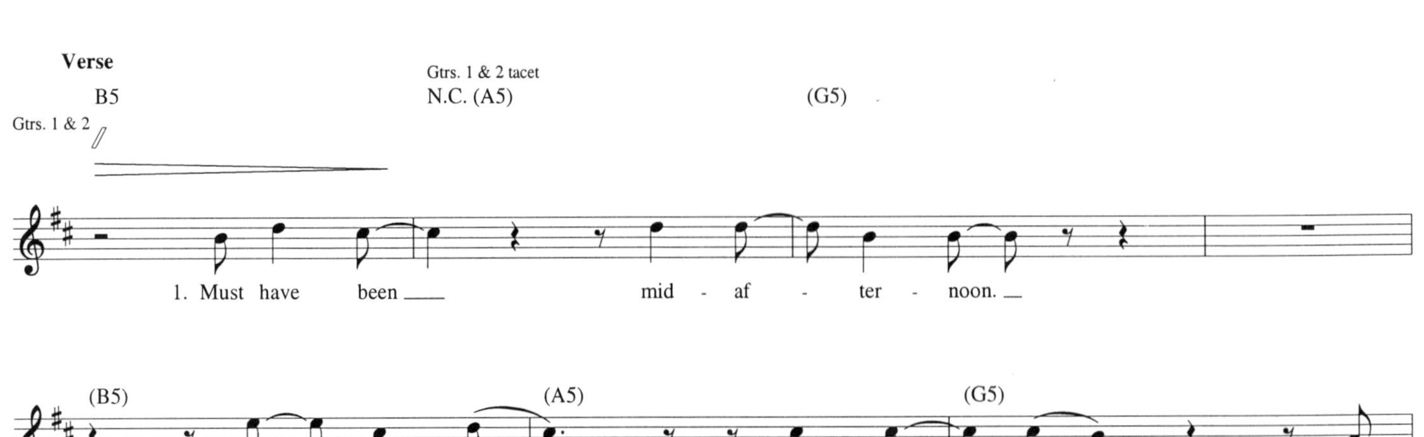

End Rhy. Fig. 1A

(cont. in slash)

Chorus

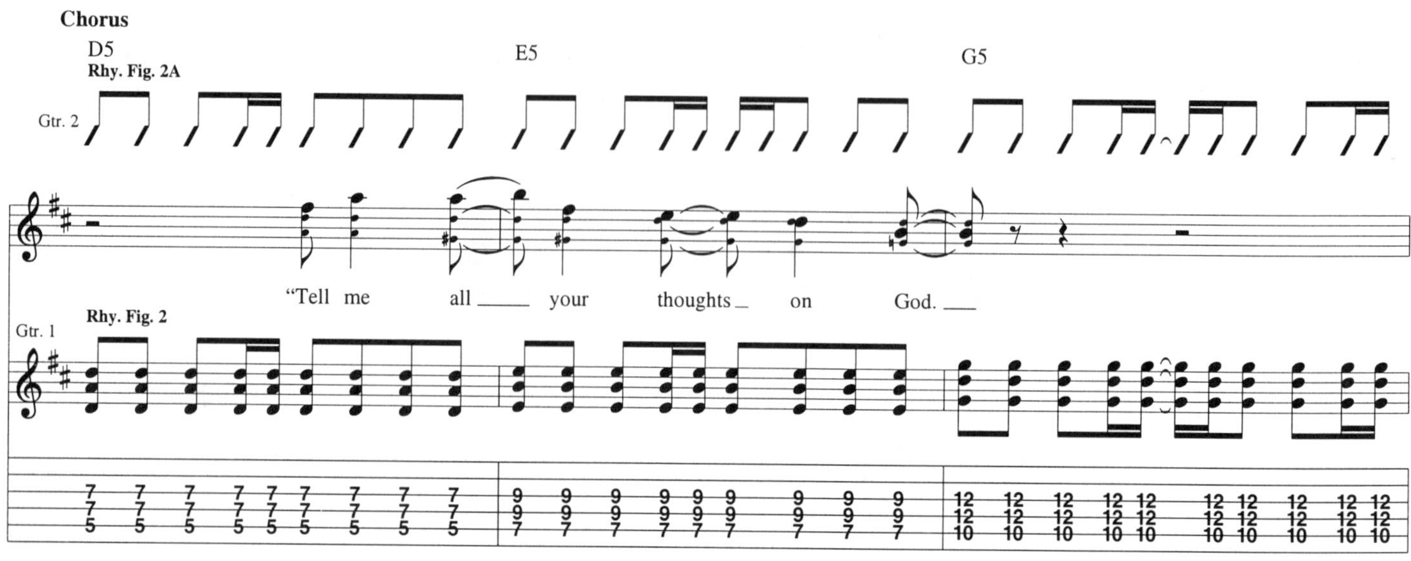

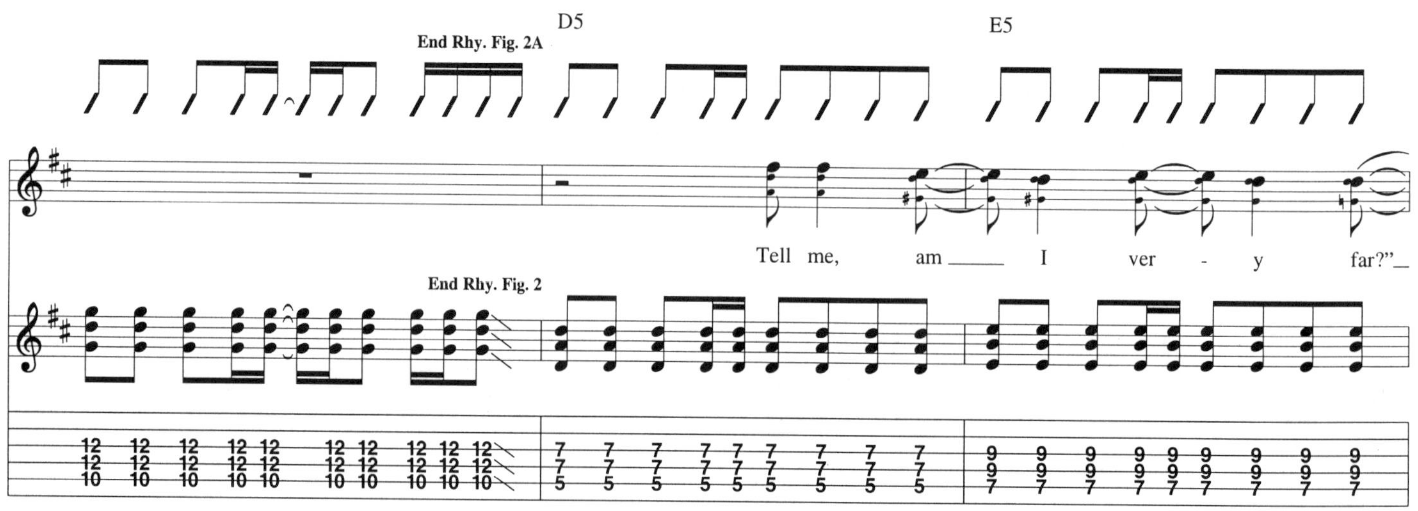

Verse

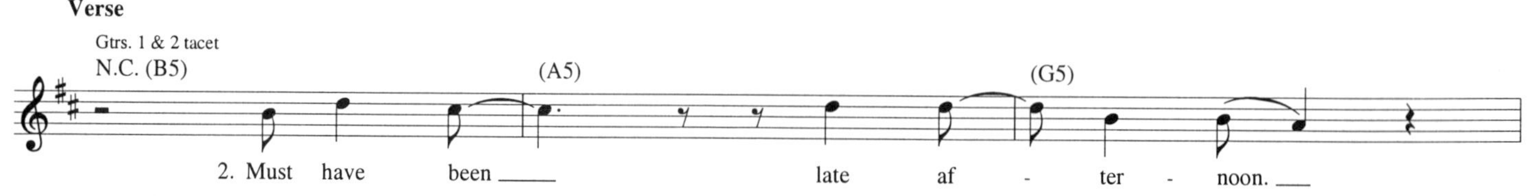

(B5)
(A5)
(G5)
On our way the sun broke free of the clouds.
Gtr. 1
8va
loco
fdbk.
1/2
1/2

Gtrs. 1 & 2: w/ Rhy. Figs. 1 & 1A, simile
Gtr. 2: w/ Rhy. Fill 1
Bsus4
E5/A
D6sus2/G
And we count only blue cars, skip the cracks in the street and ask

Bsus4
E5/A
D5/G
man - y ques - tions, like chil - dren of - ten do. We said,

Chorus

Gtrs. 1 & 2: w/ Rhy. Figs. 2 & 2A, 4 times, simile
D5
E5
G5
"Tell me all your thoughts on God, 'cause I'd real-ly like to meet her.

D5
E5
G5
And ask her why we're who we are. Oo.

D5
E5
G5
Tell me all your thoughts on God, 'cause I'm on

D5
E5
G5
my way to see her. So, tell me, am I ver - y far?

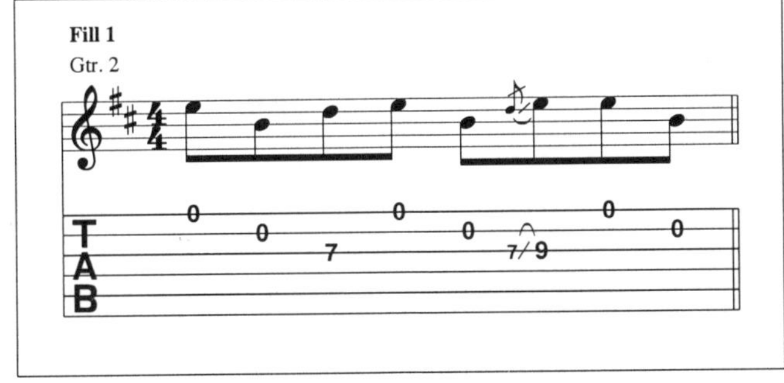
Fill 1
Gtr. 2
T
A
B

Guitar Solo
B5
A5
Am I ver - y far now?"
Gtr. 3 (elec.)
f
w/ dist.
Rhy. Fig. 3
Gtrs. 1 & 2

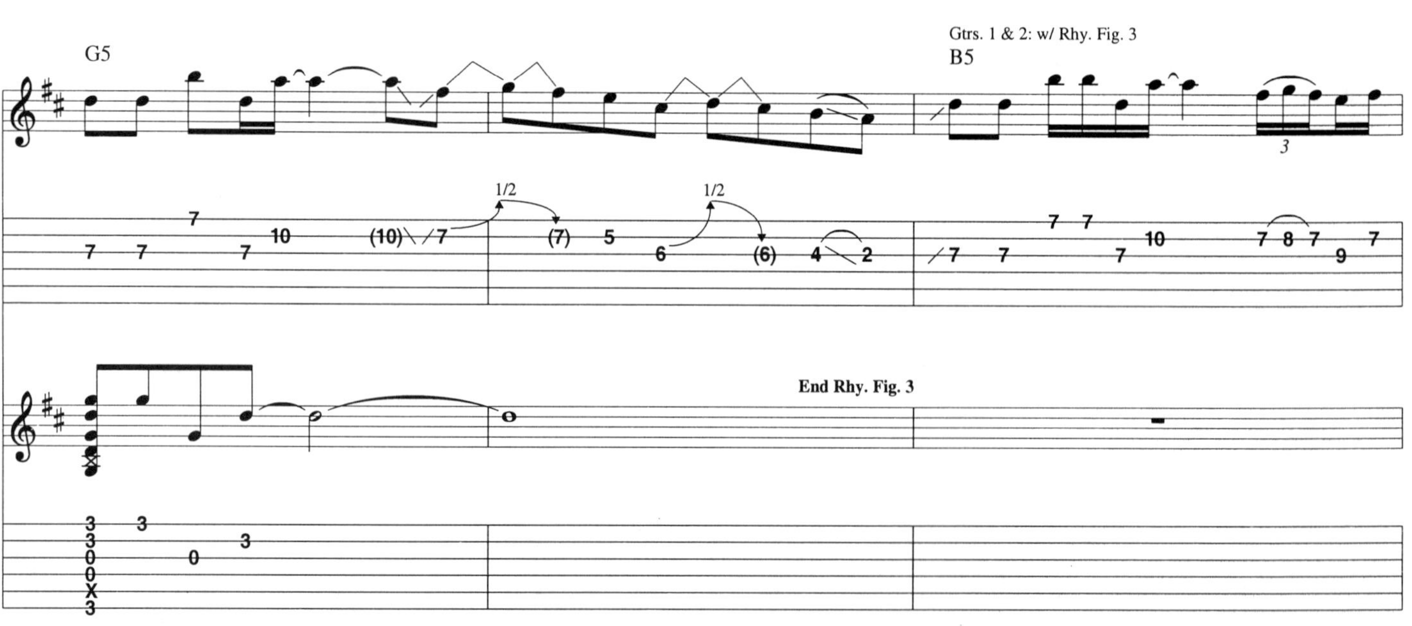
G5
Gtrs. 1 & 2: w/ Rhy. Fig. 3
B5
1/2
1/2
End Rhy. Fig. 3

A5
G5
Gtr. 3
1/2
1/2
1/2

Verse

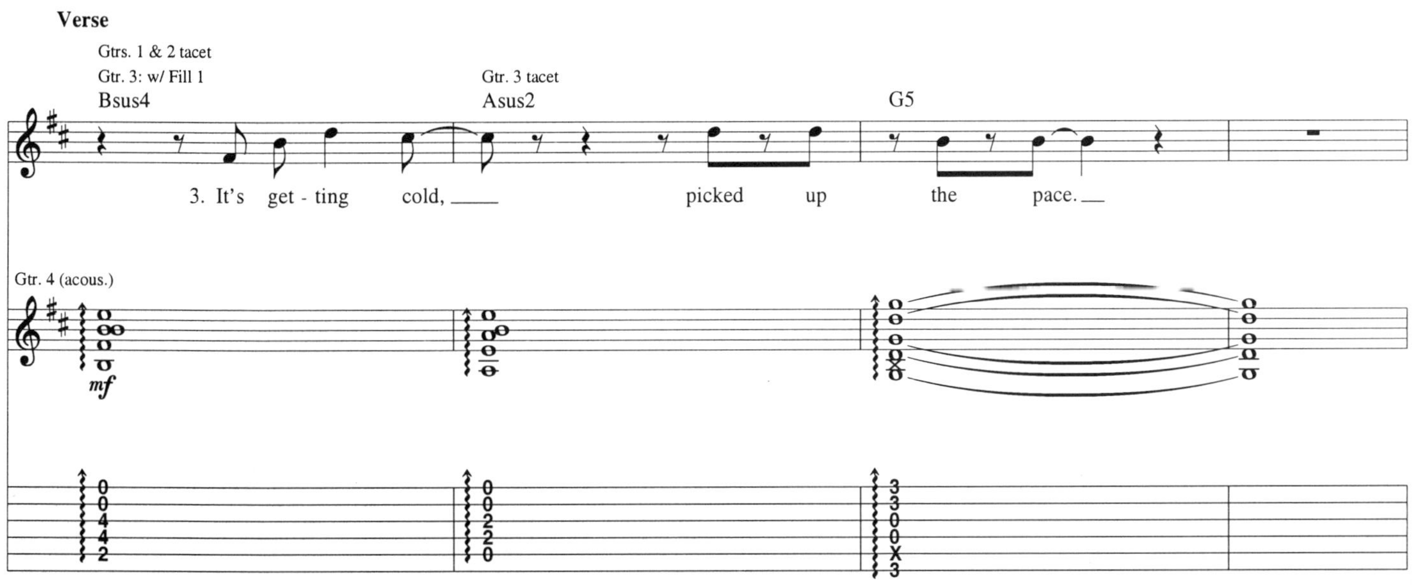
Gtrs. 1 & 2 tacet
Gtr. 3: w/ Fill 1
Gtr. 3 tacet
Bsus4
Asus2
G5
3. It's get - ting cold, picked up the pace.
Gtr. 4 (acous.)
mf

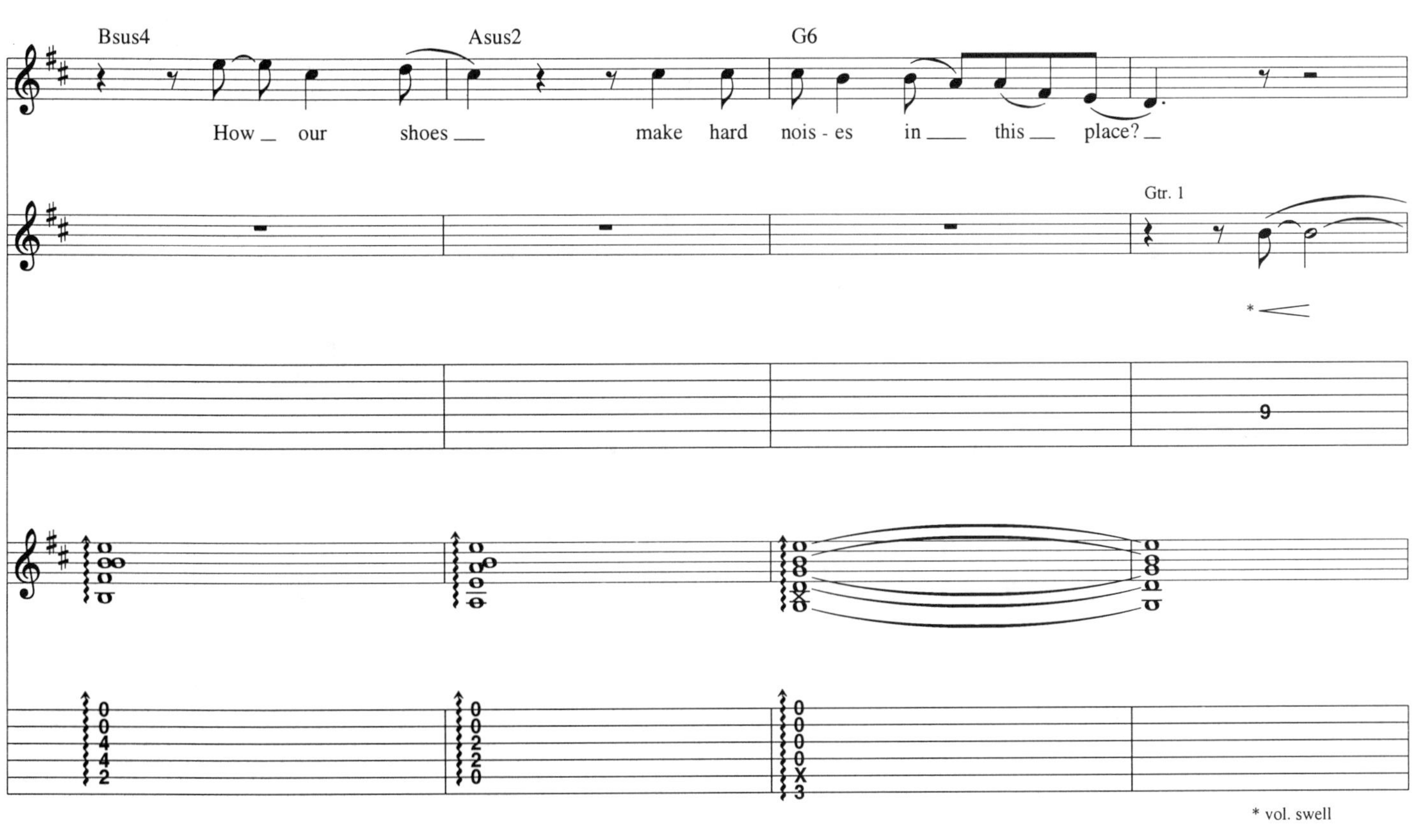
Bsus4
Asus2
G6
How our shoes make hard nois - es in this place?
Gtr. 1
* vol. swell

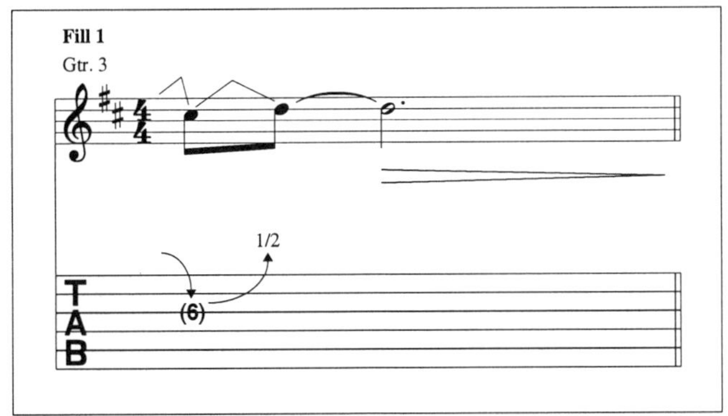
Fill 1
Gtr. 3
1/2
(6)
T
A
B

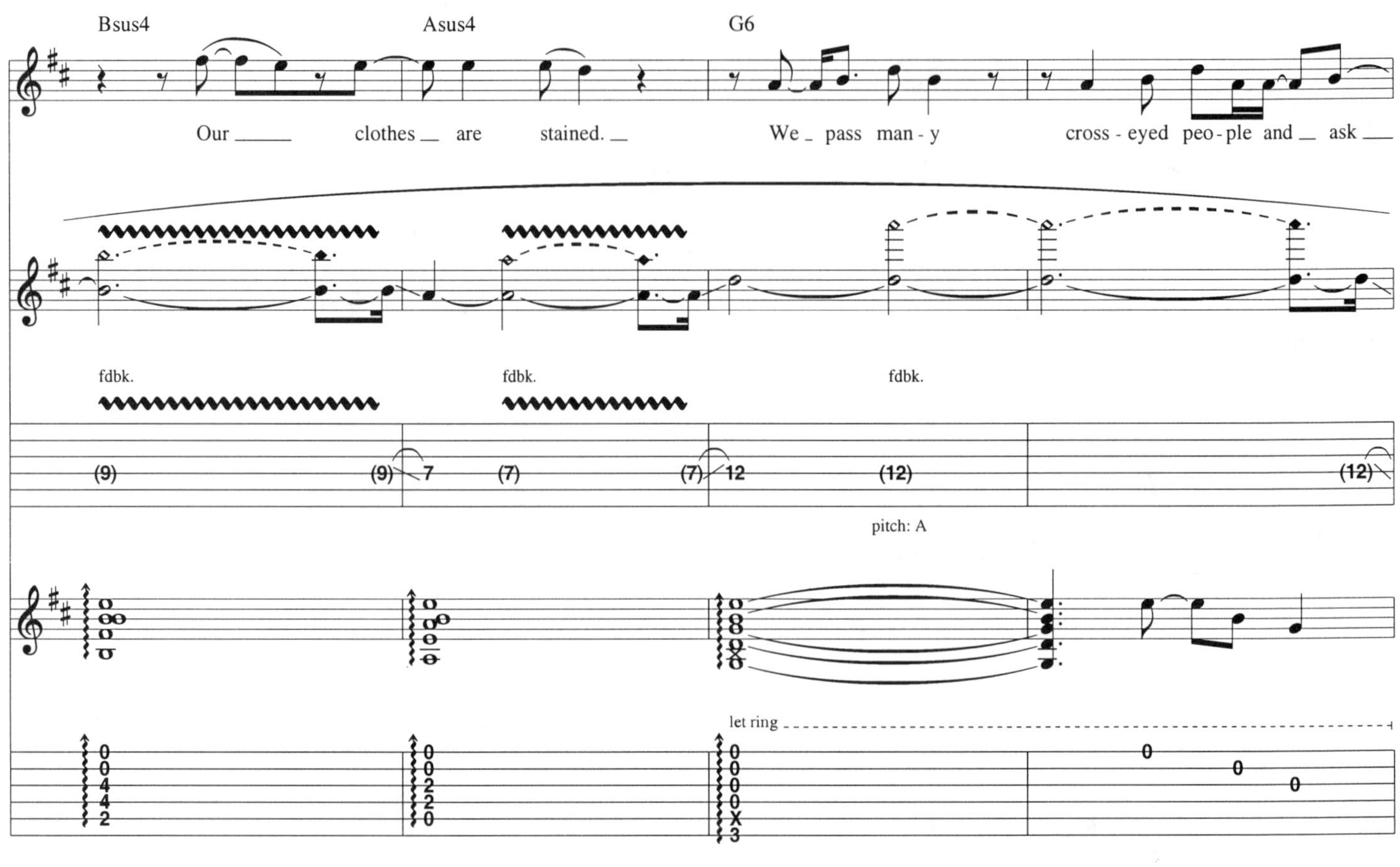

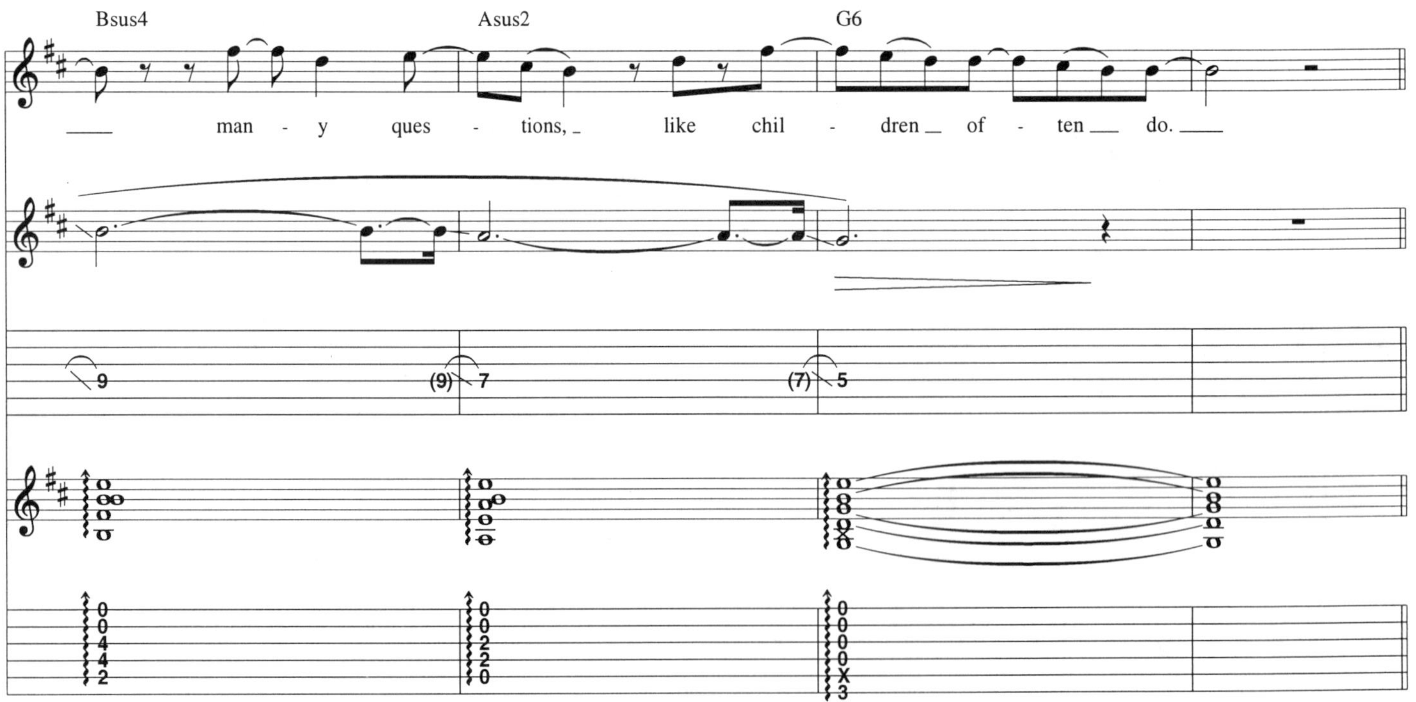

Chorus

Gtr. 1: w/ Rhy. Fig. 2, 4 times, simile
Gtr. 2: w/ Rhy. Fig. 2A, 1 3/4 times, simile
Gtr. 4 tacet

D5 E5 G5

Tell me all ___ your thoughts ___ on God, ___ 'cause I'd real - ly like ___ to meet ___ her. ___

D5
E5
G5
And ask her why we're who we are.
Oo.
D5
E5
Tell me all your thoughts on God,
Gtr. 2
Gtr. 3
G5
D5
'cause I'm on my way to see her.
So, tell me, am

E5
G5
I very - y far? Am I ver - y far
Outro
Gtrs. 1 & 2: w/ Rhy. Figs. 2 & 2A, 3 times, simile
Bkgd. Voc.: w/ Voc. Fig. 1, 3 times
D5
E5
G5
now? Am I ver - y far now? Am I ver - y far now?
Gtr. 3
1/2
1/2
D5
E5
Oo, oo, oo, oo.
Voc. Fig. 1
(Tell me all your thoughts on God.)

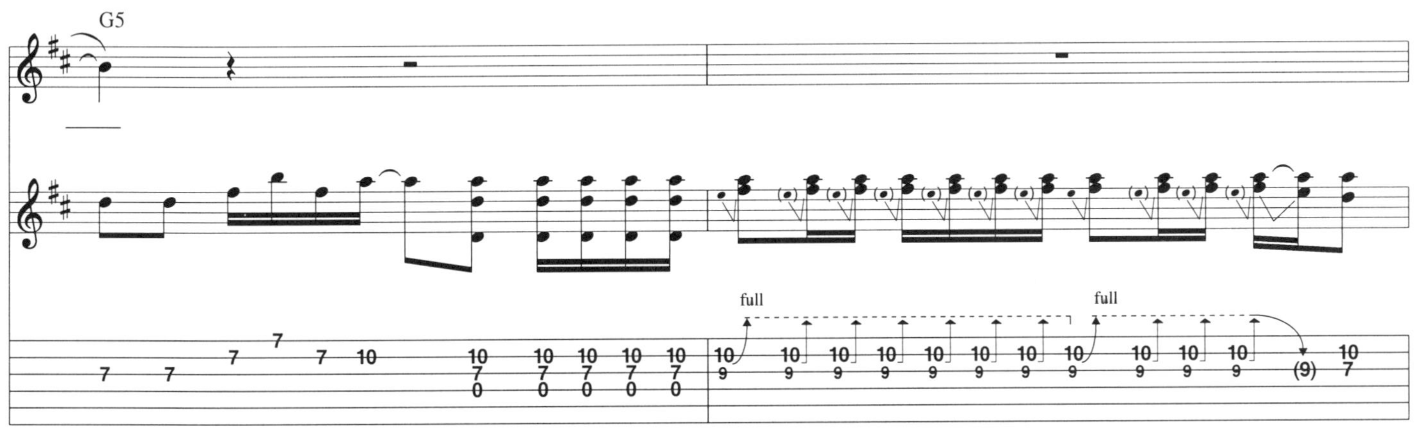
G5
full
full

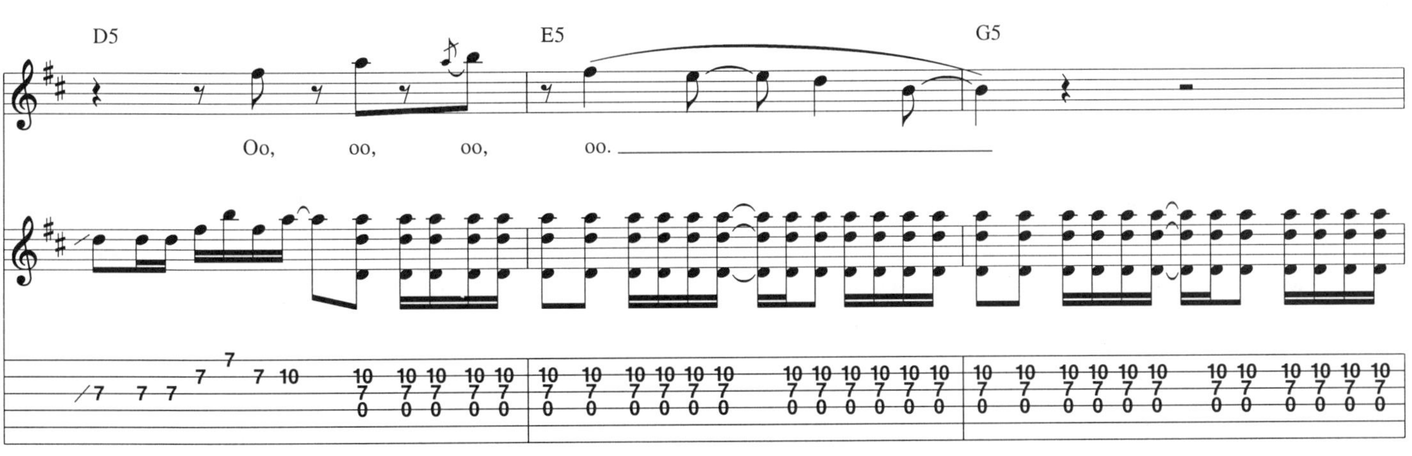
D5
E5
G5
Oo, oo, oo, oo.

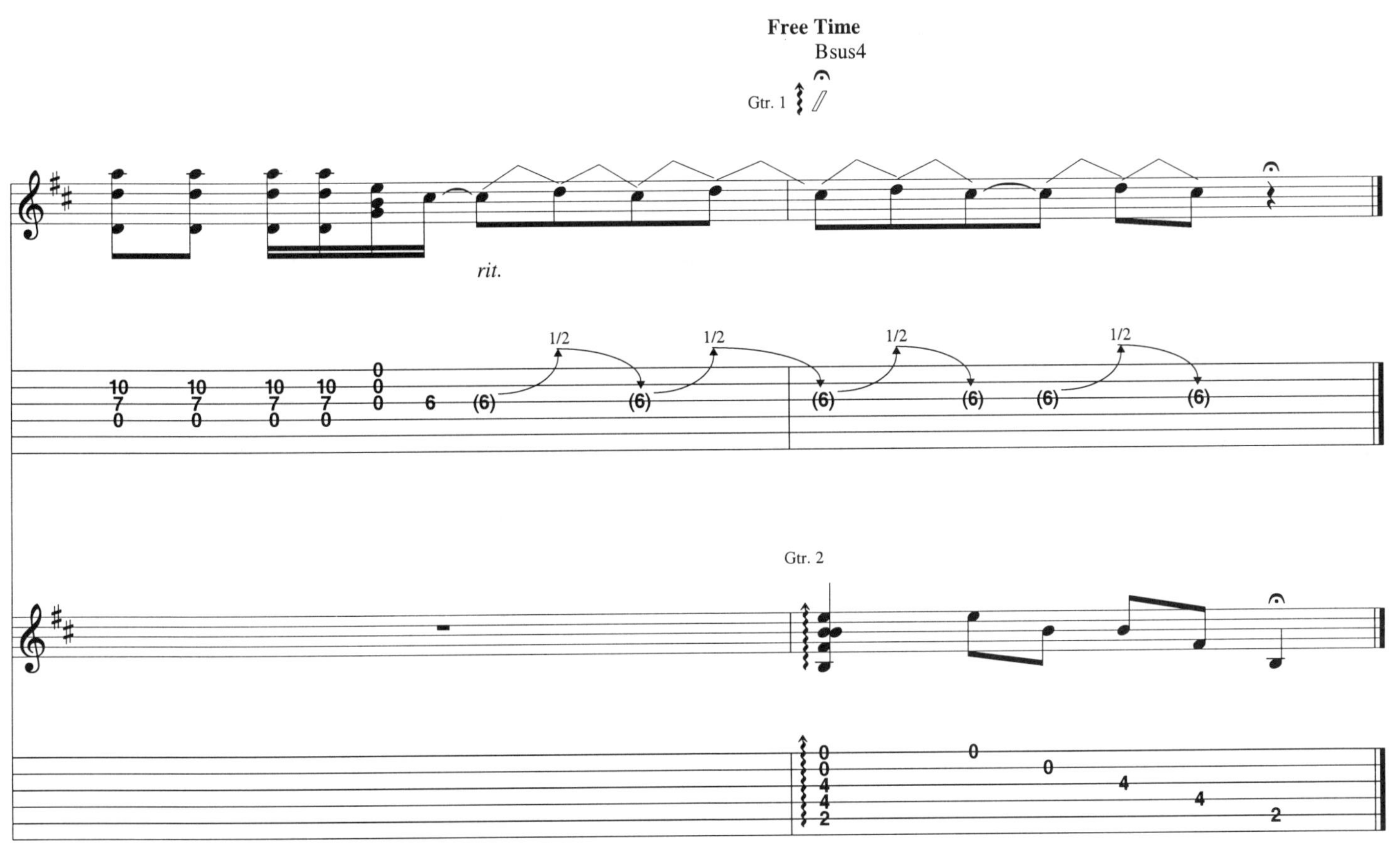
Free Time
Bsus4
Gtr. 1
rit.
1/2
1/2
1/2
1/2
Gtr. 2

Give Me One Reason

Words and Music by Tracy Chapman

* Played ahead of the beat.

Verse
Gtr. 1: w/ Rhy. Fig. 1
F♯
B
C♯
F♯
3. Give me one rea-son to stay here and I'll turn right back a - round.
1/2
1/2
1/4
B
C♯
(You can see the turn in me.)
Give me one rea-son to stay here and I'll turn right back a -
full
1/2
F♯
C♯
round.
(You can see the turn in me.)
Said I don't wan-na leave you lone - ly,
1/4
1/4
1/2
B
F♯
you got to make me change my mind.
4. I don't
3/4
1/4

Verse
Gtr. 1: w/ Rhy. Fig. 1
F♯
B
C♯
F♯
want no one to squeeze me, they might take a - way my life.
hold bend
let ring
full
12
B
C♯
I don't want no one to squeeze me, they might take a - way my
let ring
full
12 12 (12) 10 12 10 11
* Played behind the beat.
F♯
C♯
life. I just want some-one to hold me,
9 11 9
9 9 9 7 9 7
9 9 7 9 7
9
8
B
F♯
oh, and rock me through the night.
(8) 6
1/2
1/4
4 4 4 4 2
4 4 6 5 7 7

Guitar Solo

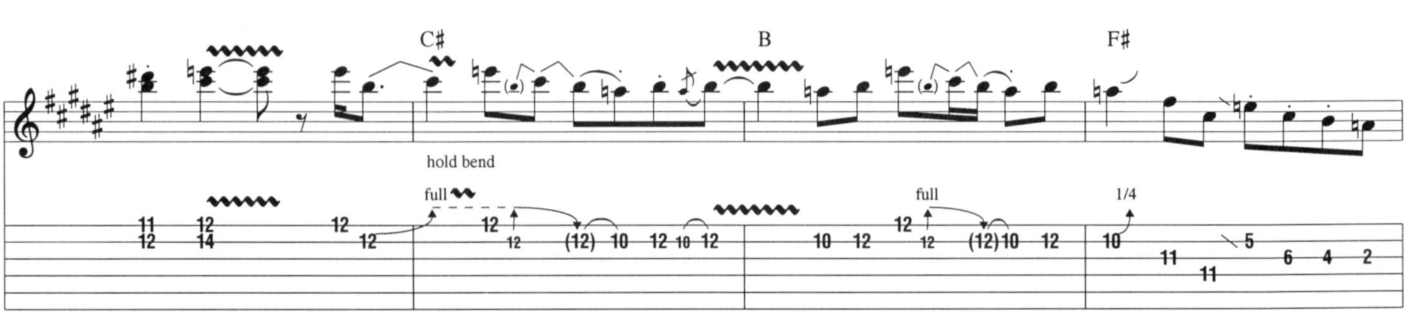

Verse

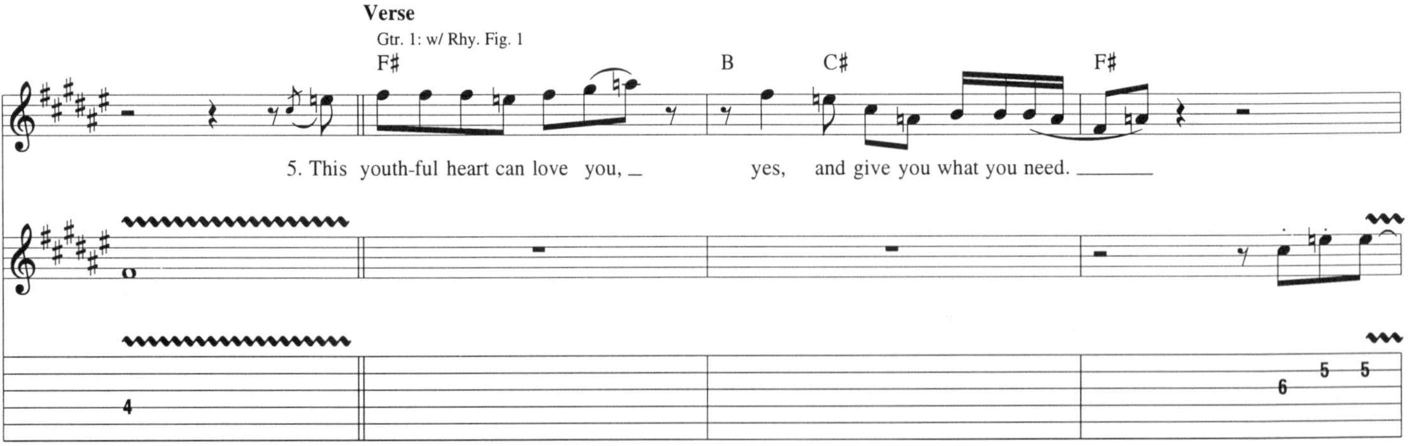

C♯
C♯7
B7
F♯
But I'm too old to go chas-in' you a-round, wast-in' my pre-cious en-er-gy.
1/4
Verse
Gtr. 1: w/ Rhy. Fig. 1
F♯
B
C♯
6. Give me one rea-son to stay here, yes, now turn right back a-round. (A -
1/4
F♯
B
round. You can see the turn in me.)
Give me one rea-son to stay here
full
1/2
1/2
full
C♯
F♯
oh, I'll turn right back a - round.
Said I
(You can see the turn in me.)
full
Gtr. 2 tacet
C♯
B
don't wan-na leave you lone - ly, you got to make me change my

Verse
Gtr. 1: w/ Rhy. Fig. 1, 1st 8 meas.
F♯
mind.
7. Ba-by, just give me one rea - son,
Gtr. 2
full
full
1/4
1/2
B
C♯
F♯
oh, give me just one rea-son why.
Ba-by, just give me one rea - son,
1/2
1/2
oh, give me just one rea - son why, I should stay.
Said I
told you that I loved you,
and there ain't no more to say.
rit.
Gtr. 1

Hold My Hand

Words and Music by Darius Carlos Rucker, Everett Dean Felber, Mark William Bryan and James George Sonefeld

Bsus2
E
take the world to-geth-er,
we'll take 'em by the hand.
let ring
(cont. in slash)
Pre-Chorus
drums enter
F♯
Rhy. Fig. 3
Gtrs. 1 & 2
End Rhy. Fig. 3
Gtrs. 1 & 2: w/ Rhy. Fig. 3
B
'Cause I got a hand for you.
Oh.
I wan-na run with you.
Verse
Gtr. 1: w/ Rhy. Fig. 2, 3 times
Gtr. 2: w/ Fill 1
2. Yes-ter-day
-ed
I saw you stand-ing there.
and I was wast-ing time,
Your
'til I
Gtr. 2: w/ Fill 2
head was down, your eyes were red,
thought a-bout your prob-lems,
no comb had touched your hair.
I thought a-bout your crimes.
I said, "Get
Then I stood
Gtr. 1
Fill 2
Gtr. 2
TAB

Gtr. 1: w/ Rhy. Fig. 2, 2 times
Gtr. 2: w/ Fill 1
Bsus2 E Bsus2 E
up __ and let __ me see __ you smile. __ We'll
up, __ and then I screamed a - loud. __ I don't wan-na
Gtr. 2: w/ Fill 2
Bsus2 E Bsus2 E
take a walk _ to - geth - er, walk the road _ a - while." __ 'Cause, _
be part of your prob - lems, don't wan - na be part of your crowd, __ no. __
Gtr. 1
let ring
Pre-Chorus
Gtrs. 1 & 2: w/ Rhy. Fig. 3, 2 times
F# E B
I got a hand for you. __
('Cause, I got a hand for you. __)
*Lead harmony 2nd time.
F# E B
Won't you let me run __ with you. __
(I wan - na run with you. __)
Chorus
B VII E VII F# IX F#sus4 F# IX F#sus4
Rhy. Fig. 4A
End Rhy. Fig. 4A
Gtr. 3 (clean elec.)
mp
1. Want you to hold my __ hand. __
2. Want you to hold my __ hand. __
(Hold my hand. __)
Gtr. 1 & 2
Rhy. Fig. 4
End Rhy. Fig. 4

Gtr. 3: w/ Rhy. Fig. 4A, 2 times
B
E
F♯
F♯sus4
F♯
F♯sus4
I'll take you to a place where you
I'll take you to the prom - ised
(Hold my hand)
Rhy. Fig. 5
End Rhy. Fig. 5

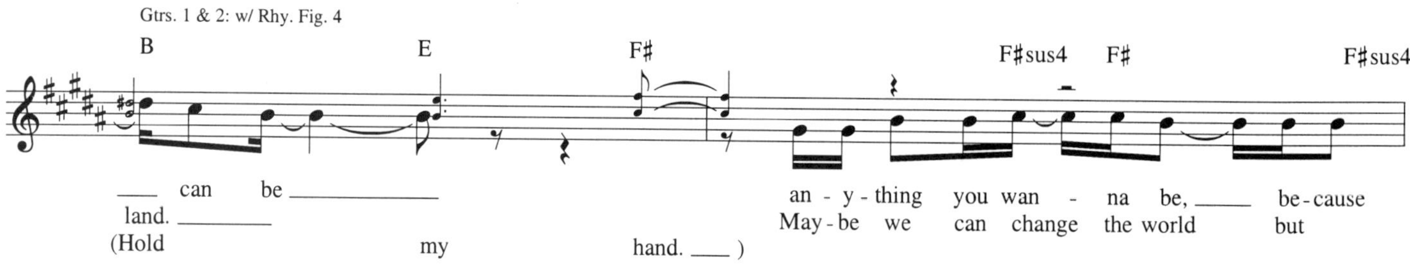
Gtrs. 1 & 2: w/ Rhy. Fig. 4
B
E
F♯
F♯sus4
F♯
F♯sus4
can be
an - y - thing you wan - na be, be-cause
land.
May-be we can change the world but
(Hold my hand.)

E[IX]
Gtr. 3
1.
I wan - na love you the best that, the best that I can.
I wan - na love you the
Gtrs. 1 & 2

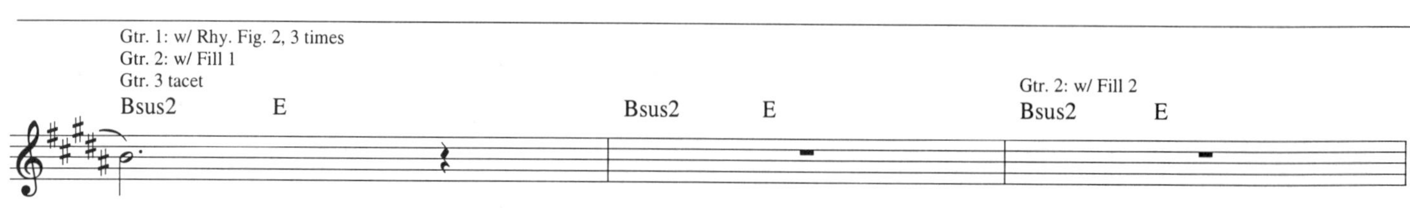
Gtr. 1: w/ Rhy. Fig. 2, 3 times
Gtr. 2: w/ Fill 1
Gtr. 3 tacet
Bsus2
E
Bsus2
E
Gtr. 2: w/ Fill 2
Bsus2
E

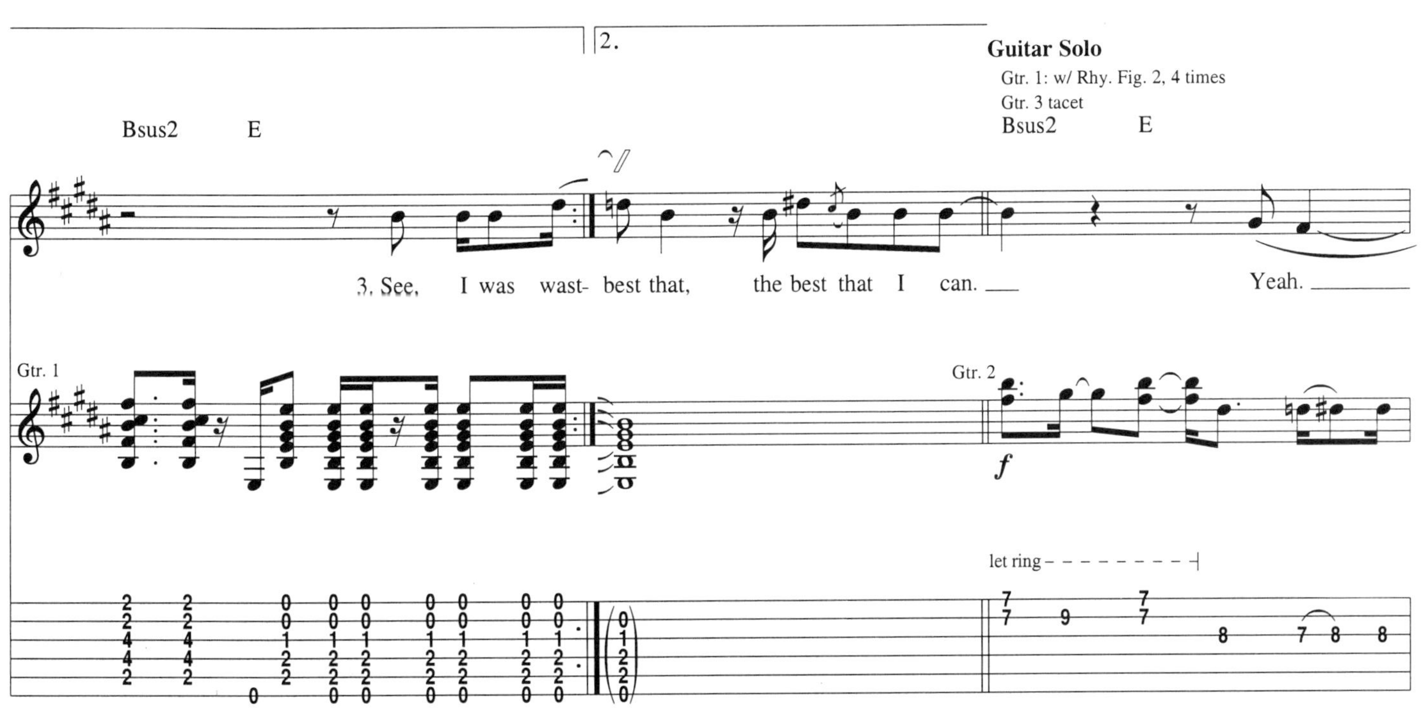
2.
Guitar Solo
Gtr. 1: w/ Rhy. Fig. 2, 4 times
Gtr. 3 tacet
Bsus2
E
3. See, I was wast- best that, the best that I can.
Yeah.
Gtr. 1
Gtr. 2
f
let ring

Bsus2
E

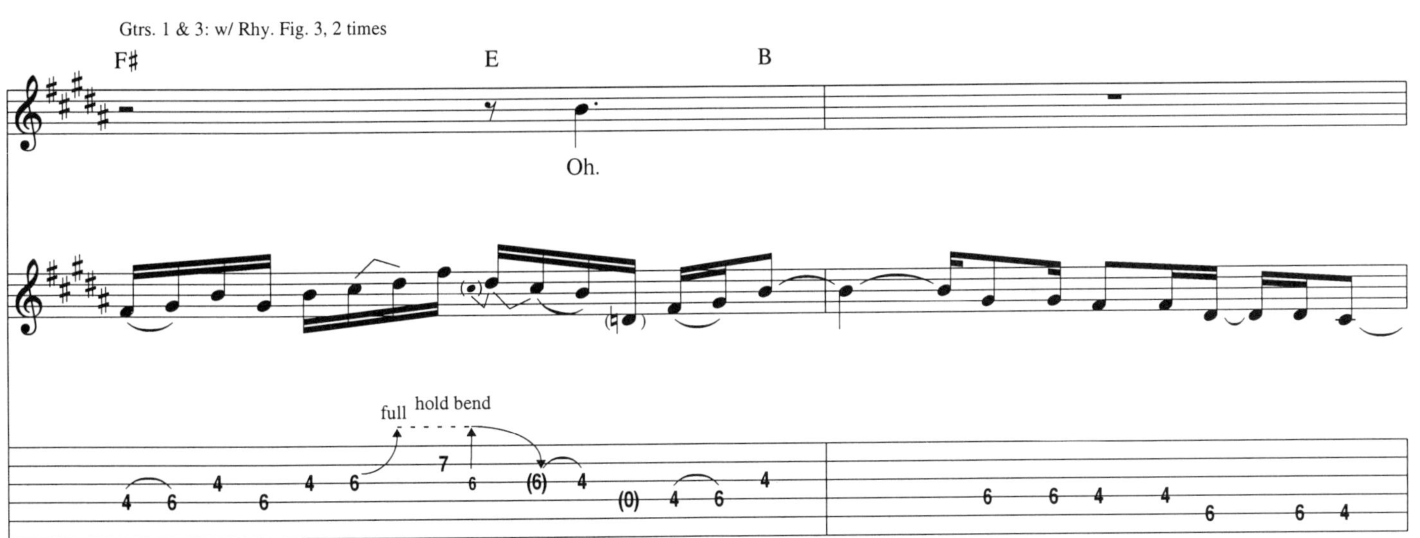
Gtrs. 1 & 3: w/ Rhy. Fig. 3, 2 times
F♯
E
B
Oh.
full
hold bend

Chorus

F♯
E
B
Let me run, won't you let me run with you.
hold bend
full

*Gtrs. 1 & 2: w/ Rhy. Fig. 4
Gtr. 3: w/ Rhy. Fig. 4A, 3 times
Gtrs. 1 & 2: w/ Rhy. Fig. 5
B
E
F♯
Want you to hold my hand.
(Hold my hand.)
(Hold my hand.
* Gtr. 2 holds notes from end of solo for two beats, then resumes with Rhy. Fig. 4

Gtrs. 1 & 2: w/ Rhy. Fig. 4
F♯7
B
E
F♯
I'll take you to a place where you can be
any-y-thing you wan - na be, be-cause
)
(Hold my hand.)

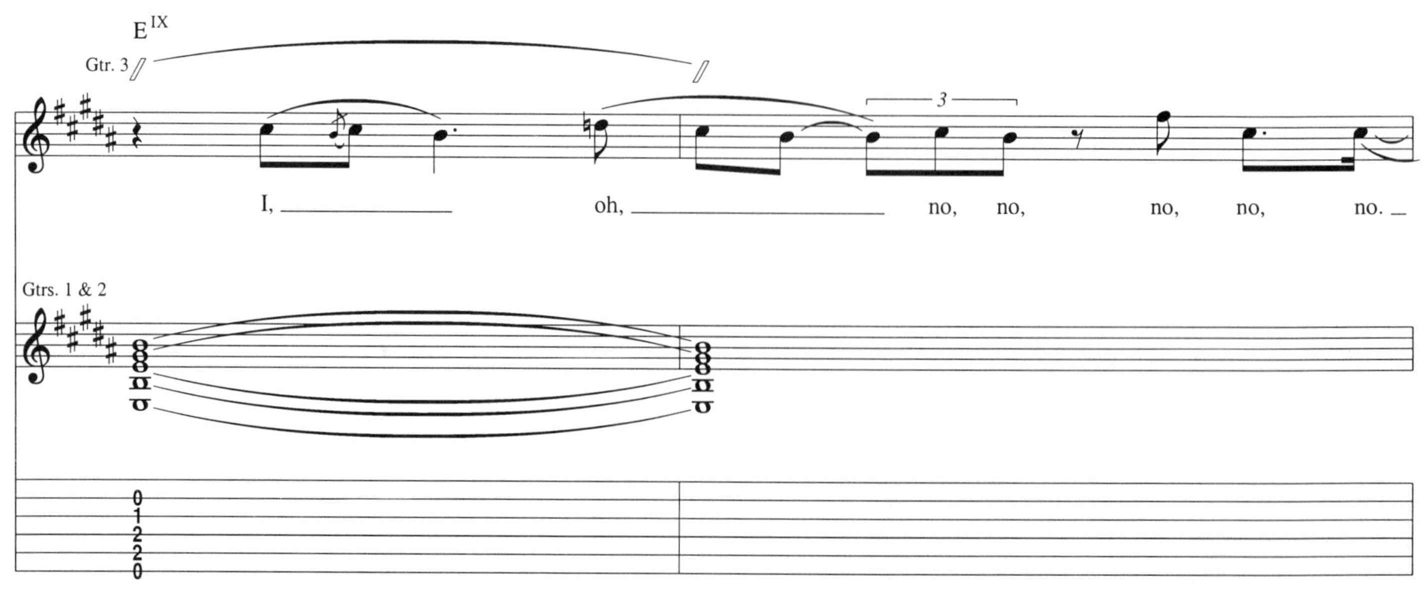

E IX
Gtr. 3
I, oh, no, no, no, no, no.
Gtrs. 1 & 2

Gtrs. 1 & 2: w/ Rhy. Fig. 4
Gtr. 3: w/ Rhy. Fig. 4A, 3 times
B E F♯
Want you to hold my hand.
(Hold my hand.)
Gtrs. 1 & 2: w/ Rhy. Fig. 5
B E F♯
(Hold my hand.
F♯7
I'll take you to the prom - ised land.
)
Gtrs. 1 & 2: w/ Rhy. Fig. 4
B E F♯
(Hold my hand.)
May-be we can't change the world, but
E IX
Gtr. 3
I wan - na love you the best that, the best that I can.
Gtrs. 1 & 2
Gtr. 1: w/ Rhy. Fig. 2, 2 times, simile
Gtr. 2: w/ Fill 1
Gtr. 3: tacet
Bsus2 E
Oh.
Bsus2 E
Best that I can.
Bsus2 E E
6 open
Bsus2 E E
6 open
Gtr. 3
Gtrs. 1 & 2

I Alone

Words and Music by Edward Kowalczyk,
Chad Taylor, Patrick Dahlheimer and Chad Gracey

Cmaj7
G
D5
C5
Cmaj7
you'll need them, your boat is at sea your
We long to be here by his re - solve a -
G D5 C5 Cmaj7 G D5 C5
an - chor is up you've been swept a - way and the great - est of teach - ers won't hes -
lone in the church, by and by to cra - dle the ba - by in space
Rhy. Fig. 2
End Rhy. Fig. 2
Cmaj7
Gtrs. 1 & 2 tacet
B5
G5
- i - tate to leave you there by your - self chained to fate
and leave you there by your - self chained to fate, yeah
*Gtr. 3 (dist.)
f
*doubled throughout
Chorus
E B5 G5 E B5 G5
I a - lone love you I a - lone tempt you
Rhy. Fig. 3
* Bkgd. vocals 2nd & 3rd time only.

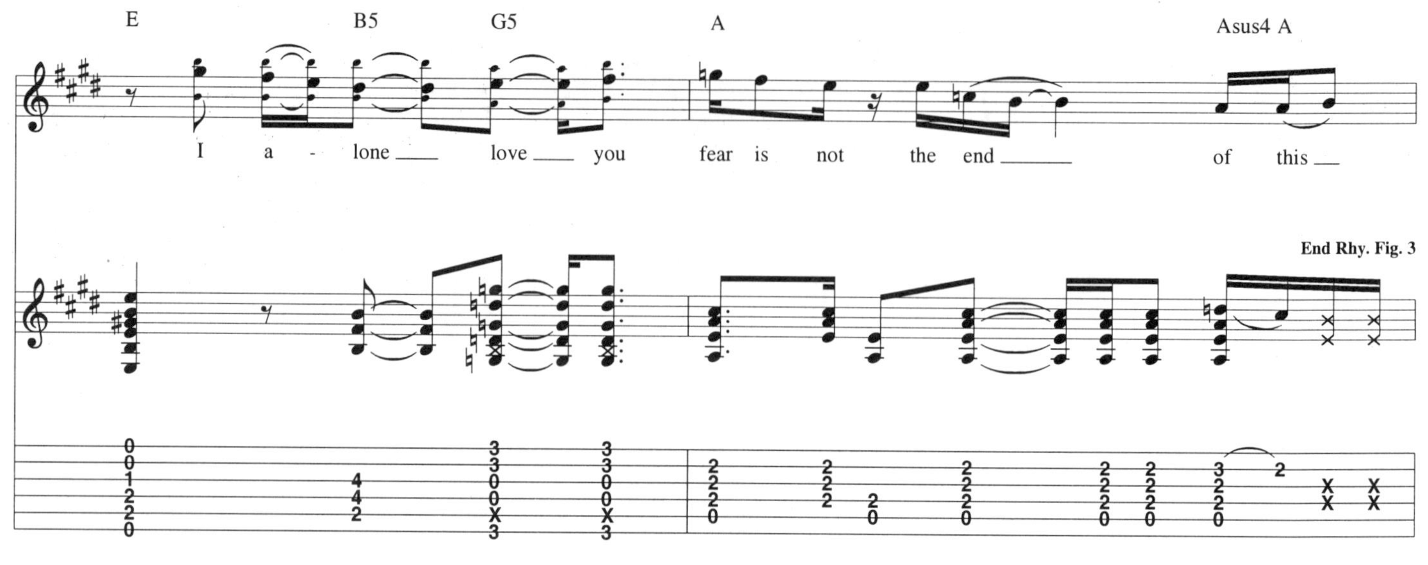

E
B5
G5
A
Asus4 A
I a - lone love you fear is not the end of this
End Rhy. Fig. 3

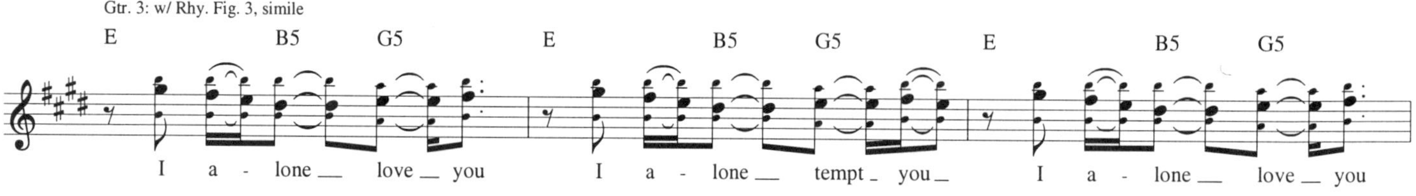

Gtr. 3: w/ Rhy. Fig. 3, simile
E
B5
G5
I a - lone love you I a - lone tempt you I a - lone love you

1.
2.
To Coda
Gtr. 3: w/ Rhy. Fig. 3, simile
A
Asus4 A
E
B5
G5
2. It's yeah. (I a - lone love you

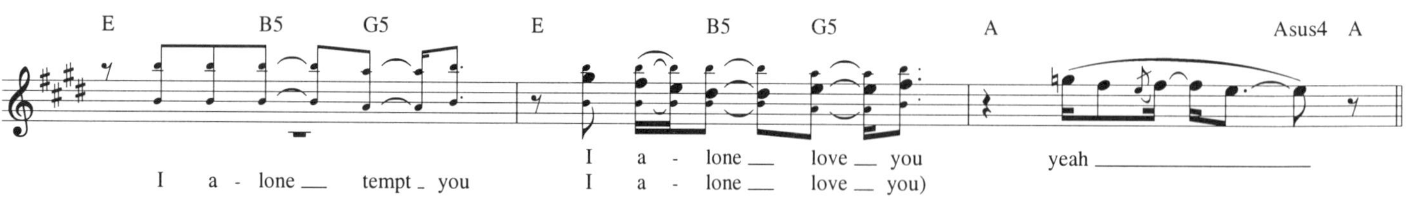

E
B5
G5
A
Asus4 A
I a - lone tempt you I a - lone love you I a - lone love you) yeah

Bridge

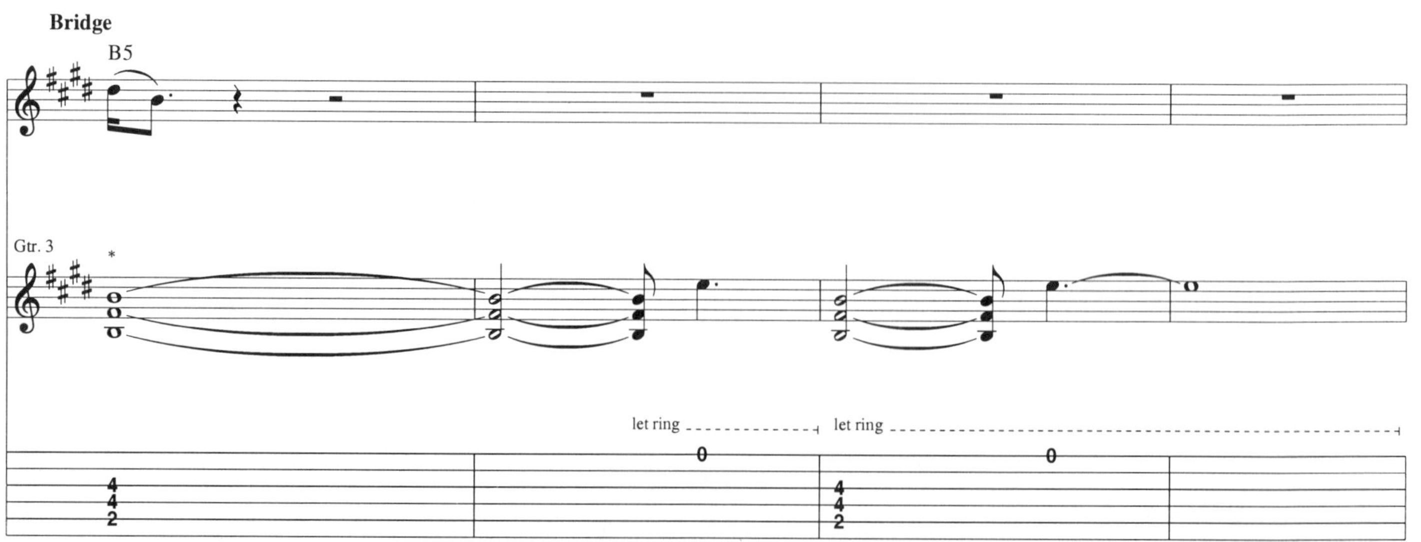

B5
Gtr. 3
let ring
let ring

*w/ fdbk. throughout section.

Oh now, we took it back _ too far only love _ can save _ us now ___ all these rid - dles that _ you
mf
burn _ all come run - nin' back _ to ___ you ___ all these rhy - thms that _ you hide _
f
only love _ can save _ us now all these rid - dles that _ you burn Yeah, yeah, yeah
D.S. al Coda
(take 2nd ending)
G
Coda
w/ Lead Voc. ad Lib.
E B5 G5 E B5 G5
Gtr. 3
(I a - lone ___ love ___ you I a - lone ___ tempt ___ you
E B5 G5
1. E B5 G5
2. E B5 G5
I a - lone ___ love _ you)
*w/ fdbk.

If You Could Only See

Words and Music by Emerson Hart

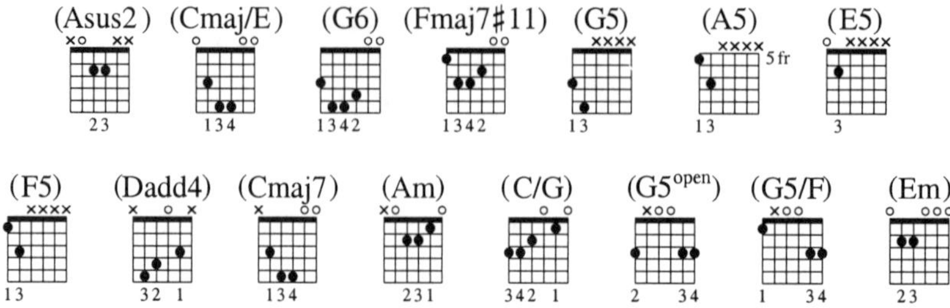

Capo I

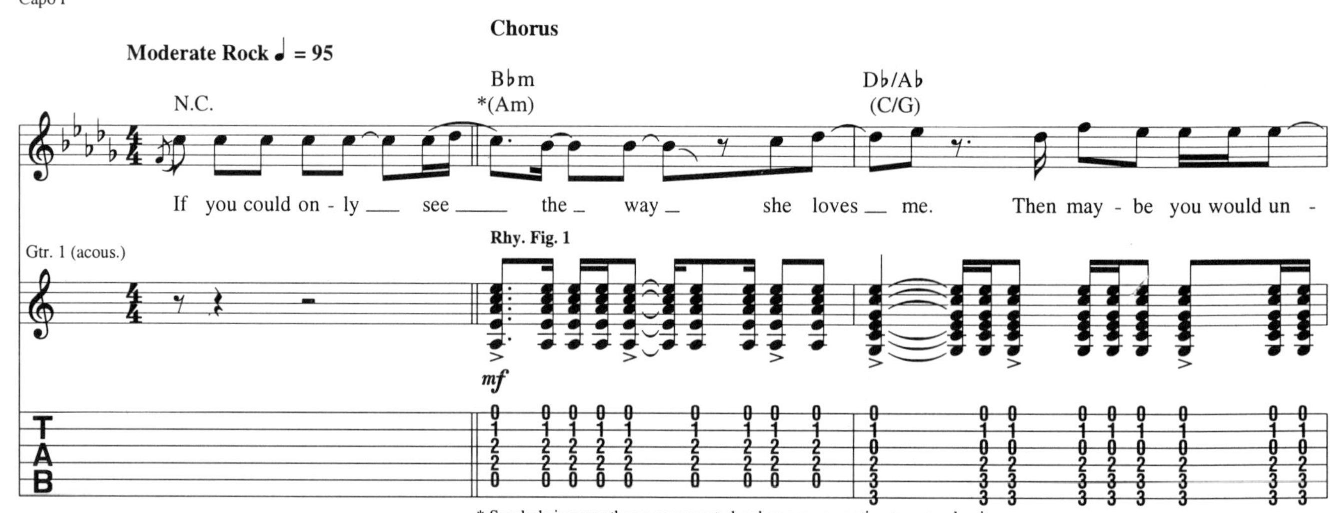

* Symbols in parentheses represent chord names respective to capoed guitar. Symbols above reflect actual sounding chord. Capoed fret is "0" in TAB.

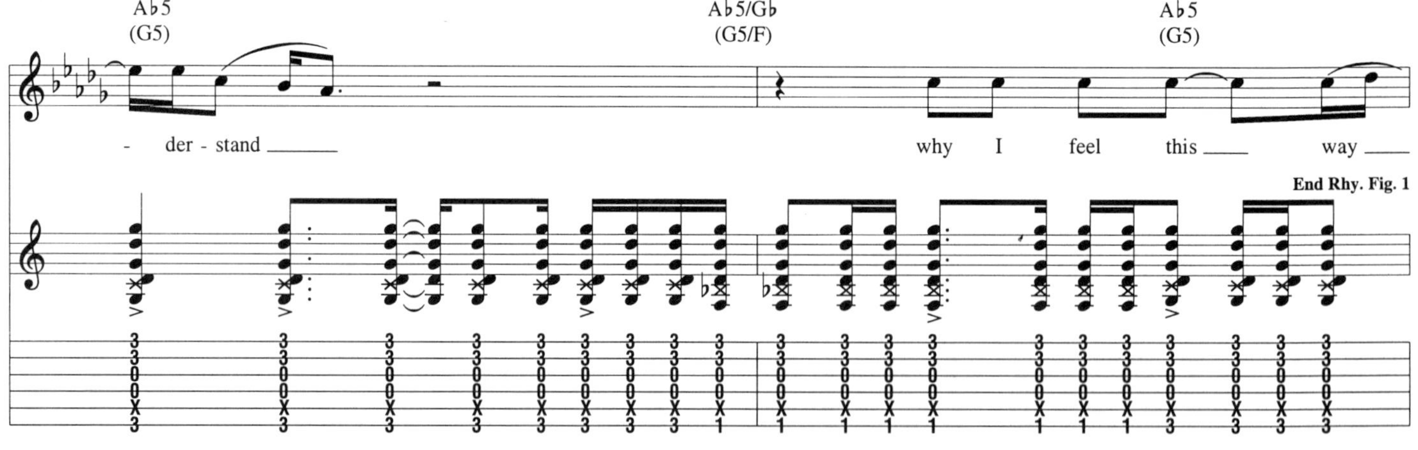

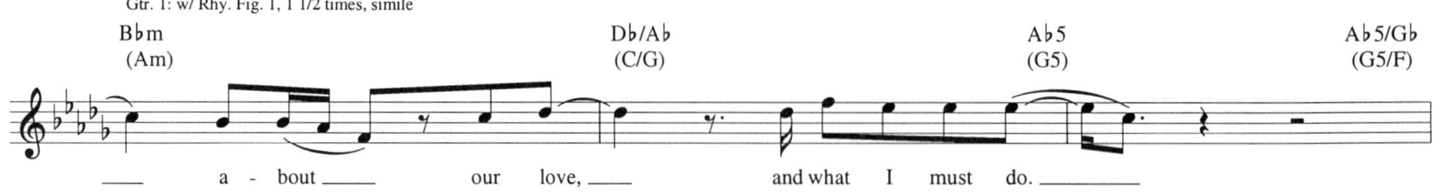

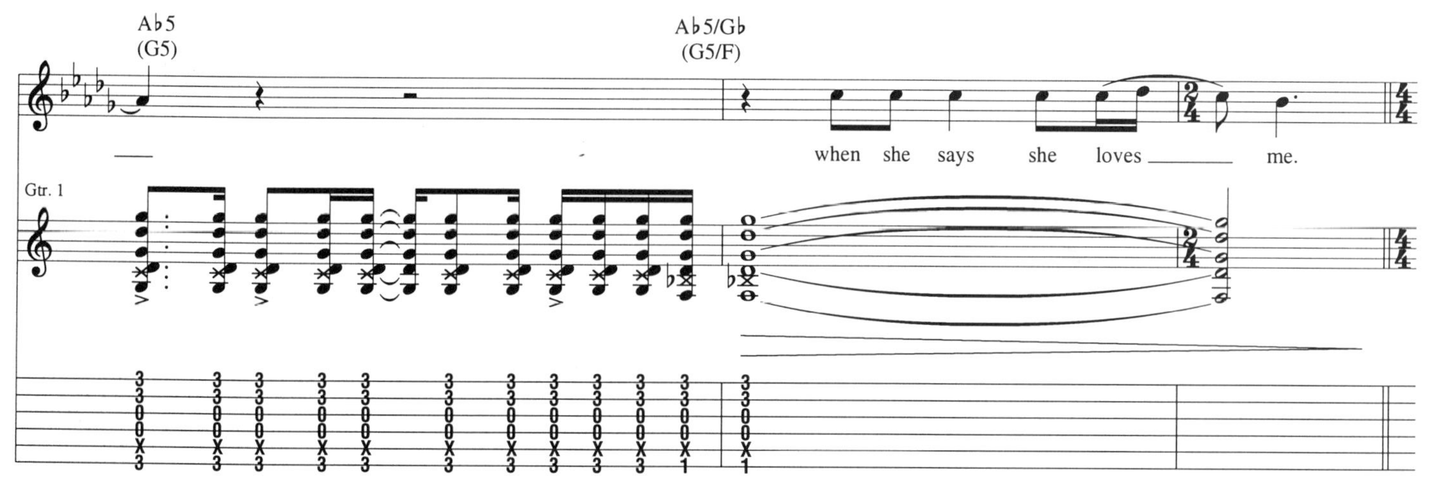

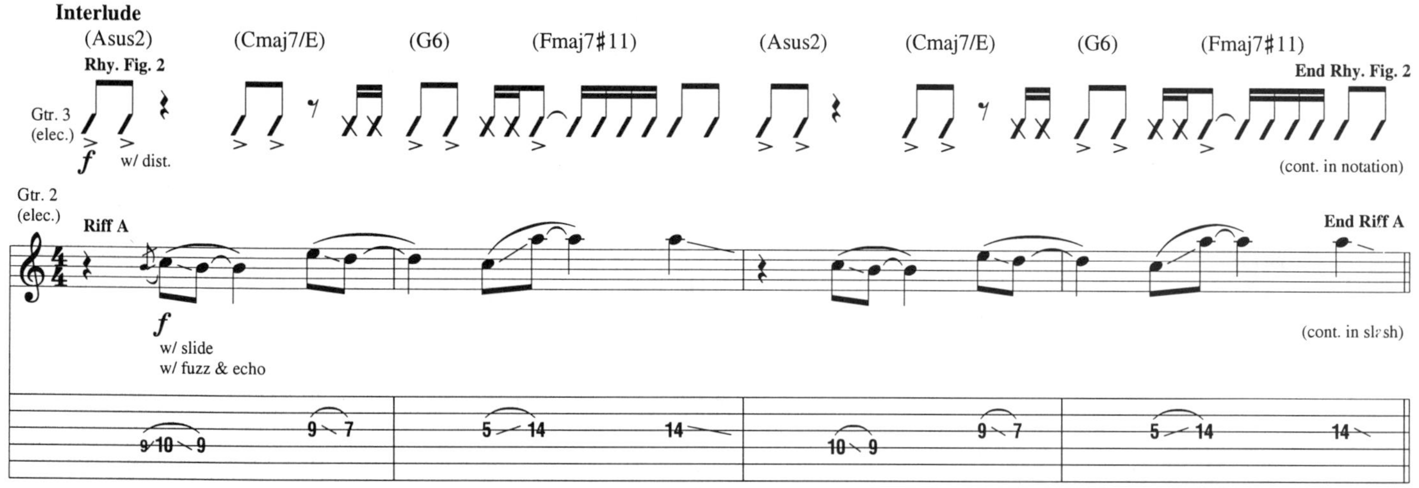

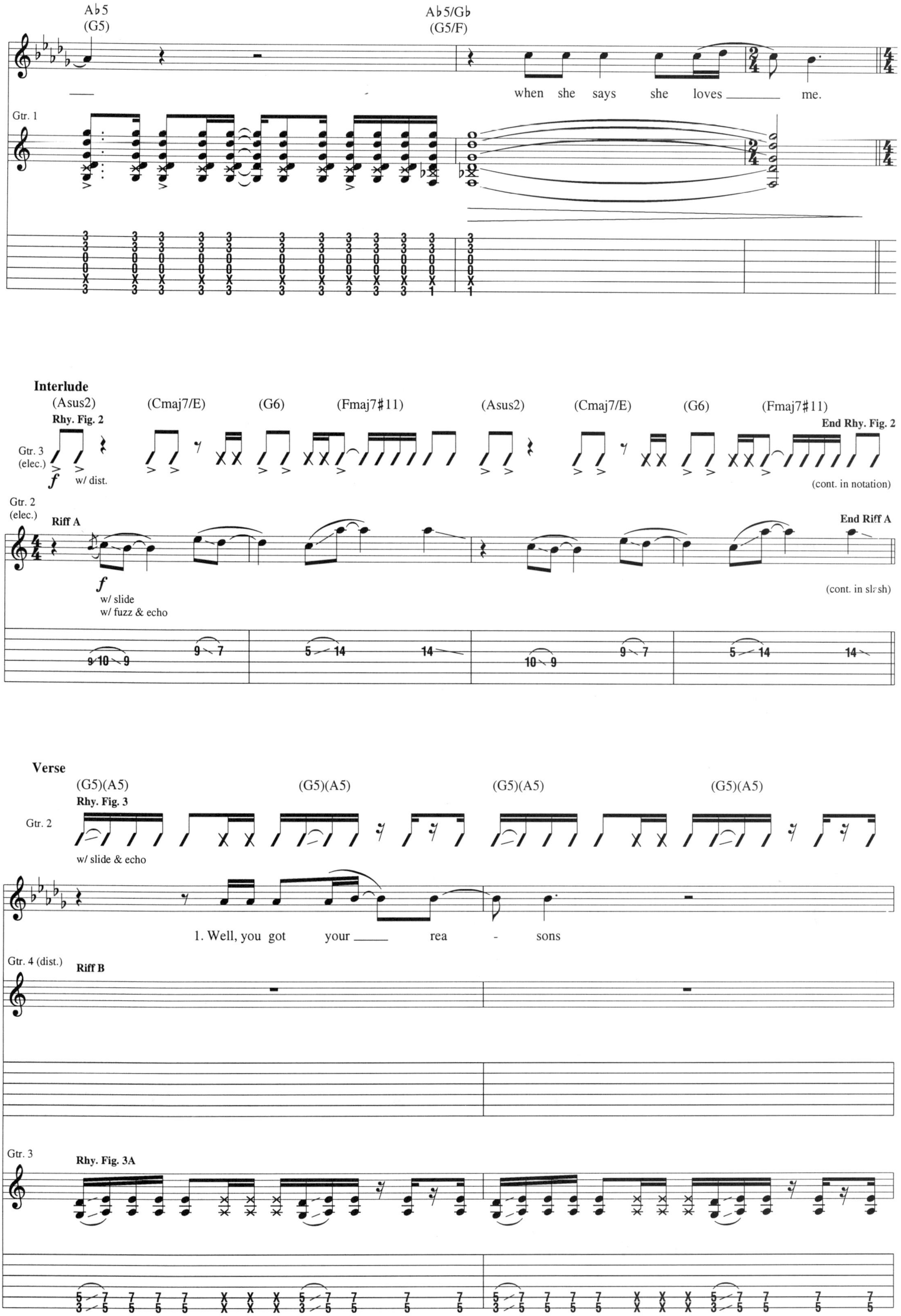

Verse

(G5)(A5) (G5)(A5) (G5)(A5) (G5)(A5)

Rhy. Fig. 3

Gtr. 2

w/ slide & echo

1. Well, you got your rea - sons

Gtr. 4 (dist.)

Riff B

Gtr. 3

Rhy. Fig. 3A

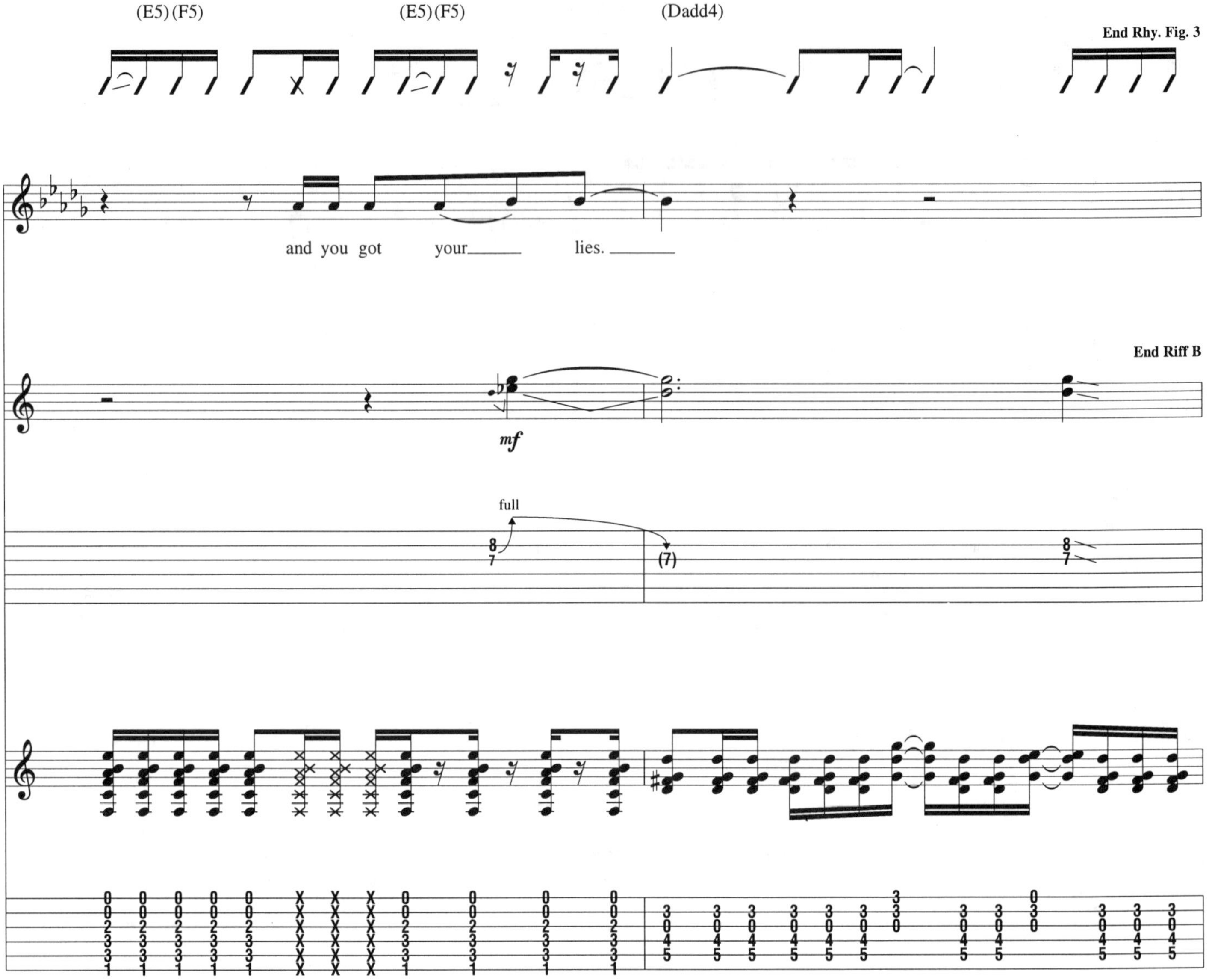

(E5) (F5)
(E5) (F5)
(Dadd4)
End Rhy. Fig. 3
and you got your lies.
End Riff B
mf
full

Gtr. 2: w/ Rhy. Fig. 3
Gtr. 4: w/ Riff B
*Ab5 Bb5
(G5)(A5)
Ab5 Bb5
(G5)(A5)
Ab5 Bb5
(G5)(A5)
Ab5 Bb5
(G5)(A5)
And you got your ma - nip - u - la - tions,
Gtr. 3

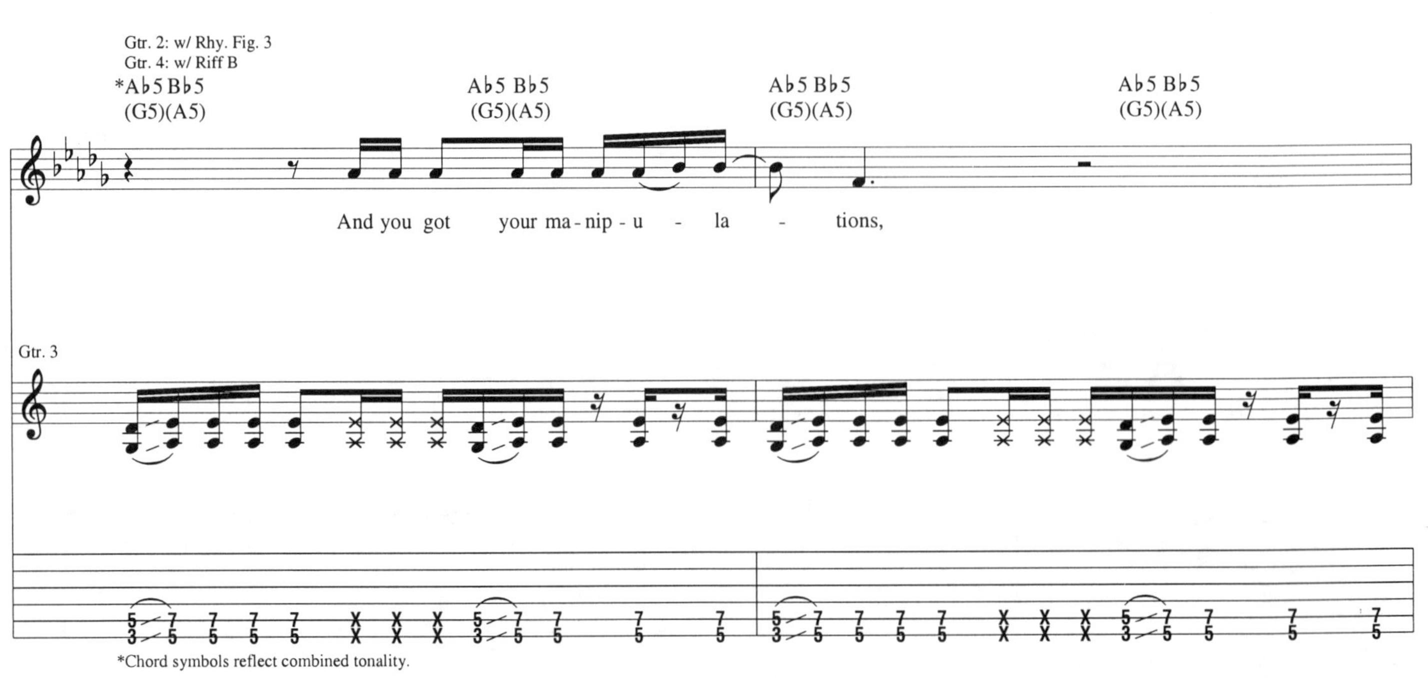

*Chord symbols reflect combined tonality.

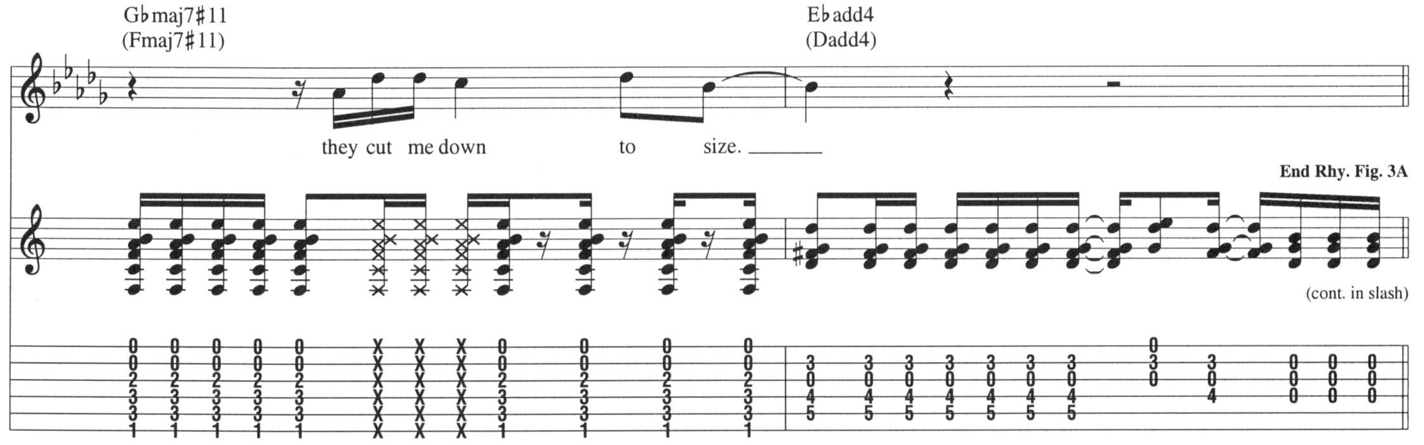
Gbmaj7#11
(Fmaj7#11)
Ebadd4
(Dadd4)
they cut me down to size.
End Rhy. Fig. 3A
(cont. in slash)

Pre-Chorus
(Asus2)
(Cmaj7)
(G6)
Gtr. 3
Say-in' you love but you don't. You give your love but you won't.
Gtr. 4
full

Chorus
Gtr. 1: w/ Rhy. Fig. 1, 3 times, 1st time; 2 3/4 times, 2nd & 3rd times
Gtr. 4 tacet
Bbm
(Am)
Db/Ab
(C/G)
If you could on - ly see the way she loves me, then may - be you would un -
Gtr. 4
Gtr. 2
Rhy. Fig. 4
w/ clean tone & delay
let ring
full
Gtr. 3
Rhy. Fig. 4A
w/ clean tone
let ring

Gtr. 5: w/ Fill 1, 3rd time
Ab5
(G5)
Ab5/Gb
(G5/F)
Ab5
(G5)
- der - stand
why I feel this way
End Rhy. Fig. 4
let ring
End Rhy. Fig. 4A
let ring
Gtrs. 2 & 3: w/ Rhy. Figs. 4 & 4A, 2 times, 1st time; 1 3/4 times, 2nd & 3rd times
To Coda 2
Bbm
(Am)
Db/Ab
(C/G)
Ab5
(G5)
Ab5/Gb
(G5/F)
Ab5
(G5)
a - bout our love, and what I must do.
If you could on - ly see
To Coda 1
Bbm
(Am)
Db/Ab
(C/G)
Ab5
(G5)
Ab5/Gb
(G5/F)
Ab5
(G5)
how blue her eyes can be when she says,
when she says she loves
Interlude
Gtr. 2: w/ Riff A
Gtr. 3: w/ Rhy. Fig. 2, simile
Bbsus2
(Asus2)
Dbmaj7/F
(Cmaj7/E)
Ab6
(G6)
Gbmaj7#11
(Fmaj7#11)
Bbsus2
(Asus2)
Dbmaj7/F
(Cmaj7/E)
Ab6
(G6)
Gbmaj7#11
(Fmaj7#11)
Verse
Gtr. 3: w/ Rhy. Fig. 3A, simile
Gtr. 2: w/ Rhy. Fig. 3, 2 times, simile
Gtr. 4: w/ Riff B, 2 times
Ab5 Bb5
(G5) (A5)
Ab5 Bb5
(G5) (A5)
me.
2. Seems the road less trav -
Gtr. 5 (elec.)
mf
w/ slide
w/ slight dist. & heavy reverb
Fill 1
Gtr. 5
TAB

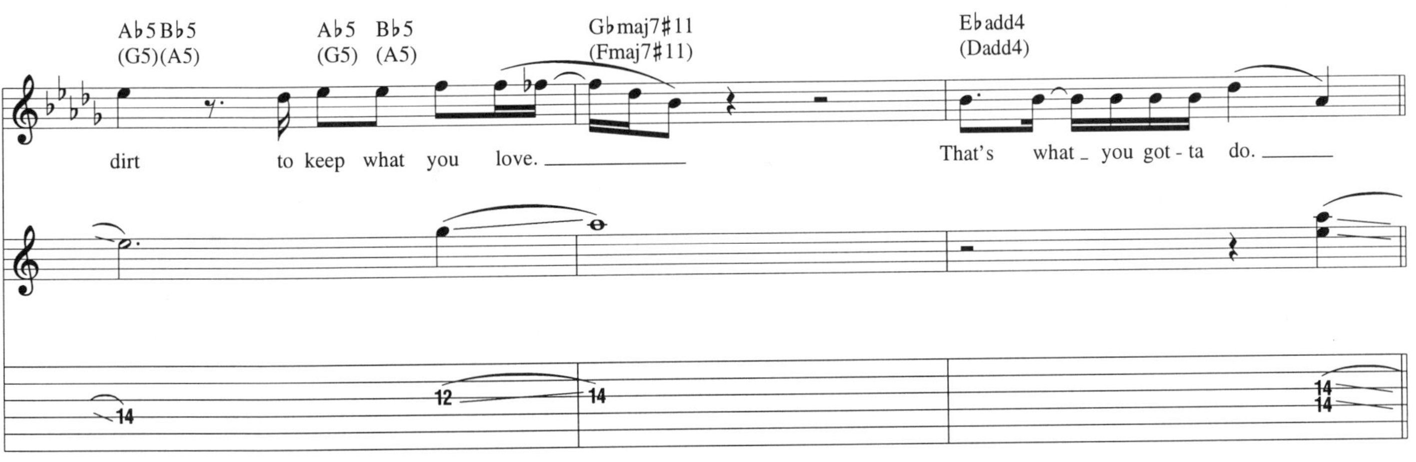

Pre-Chorus

(Am) Gtr. 1

Gtr. 5 tacet (C/G)

*Voc. Fig. 1

Say-in' you love but you don't. You give your love but you

(Oh.

Gtr. 5

Gtr. 3 Rhy. Fig. 5

* Bkgd. Voc. only

(G5 open)
(G5/F)
(G5 open)
(Am)
Gtr. 1
won't. You're stretch-ing out your arms to some-thing that's just not there.
Oh.
Say-in' you love where you
Gtr. 3
(C/G)
(G5 open)
D.S. al Coda 1
End Voc. Fig. 1
stand. Give your heart when you can.
If you could on - ly see
End Rhy. Fig. 5
Coda 1
Guitar Solo
(Em)
(E)
(Fmaj7♯11)
B
(G)
(Am)
Gtr. 5
4fr
(cont. in notation)
when she says she loves me.
Gtr. 2
Gtr. 4
full
1/2
Gtrs. 1 & 3
Rhy. Fig. 6
End Rhy. Fig. 6

Gtrs. 1 & 3: w/ Rhy. Fig. 6, 3 times, simile
F
(E)
Gbmaj7#11
(Fmaj7#11)
Ab5
(G5)
Bbm
(Am)
Gtr. 5
mf
Gtr. 4
full
Pre-Chorus
Bkgd. Voc.: w/ Voc. Fig. 1
Gtr. 3: w/ Rhy. Fig. 5
Bbsus2
(Asus2)
Dbmaj7
(Cmaj7)
Ab6
(G6)
Say-in' you love but you don't. You give your love but you won't.
Riff C
End Riff C

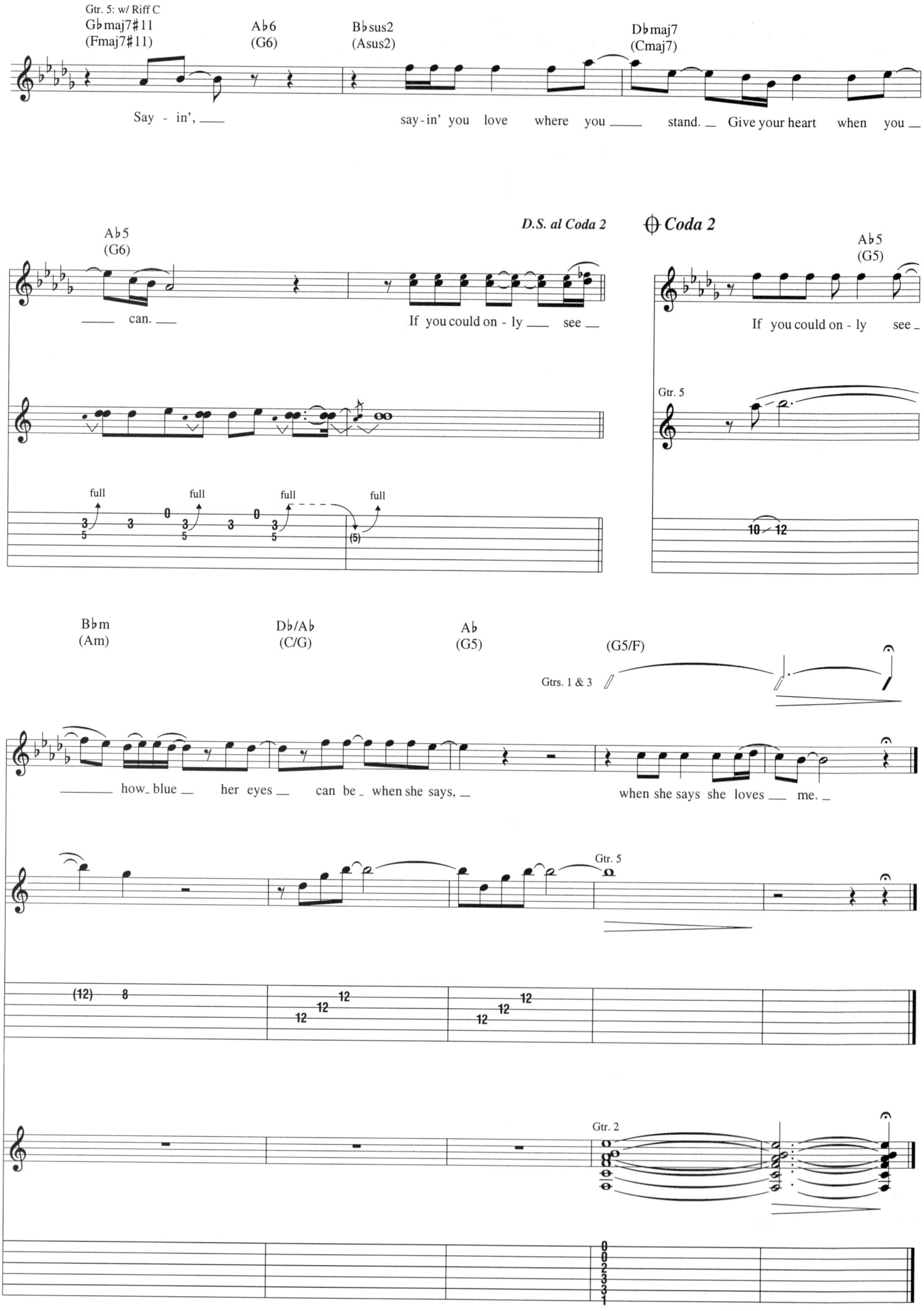

A♭5
(G6)

D.S. al Coda 2

Coda 2

A♭5
(G5)

can. If you could on - ly see

If you could on - ly see

full full full full

Gtr. 5

B♭m
(Am)
D♭/A♭
(C/G)
A♭
(G5)
(G5/F)

Gtrs. 1 & 3

how blue her eyes can be when she says, when she says she loves me.

Gtr. 5

Gtr. 2

The Impression That I Get

Words and Music by Dicky Barrett and Joe Gittleman

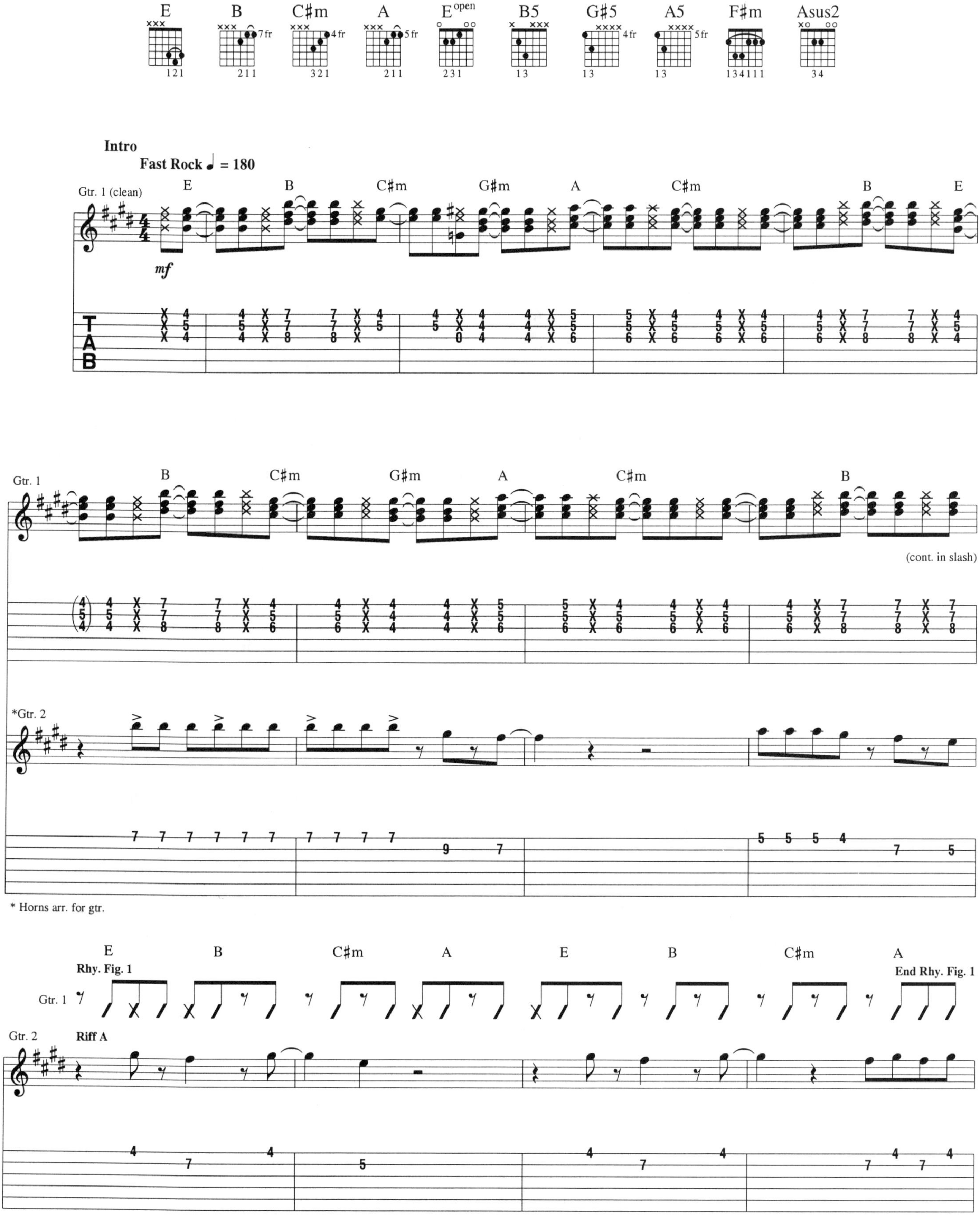

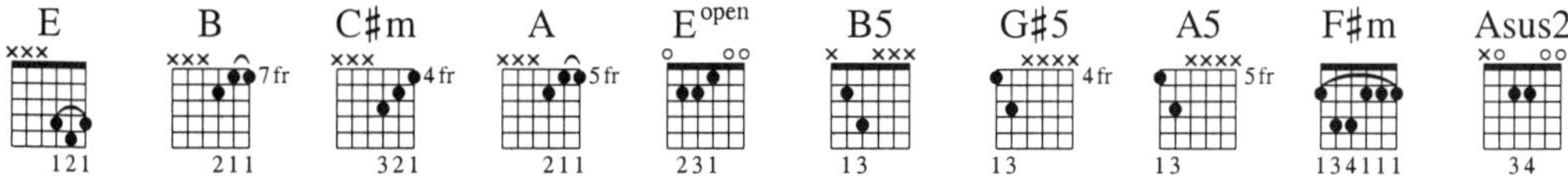

Intro

Fast Rock ♩ = 180

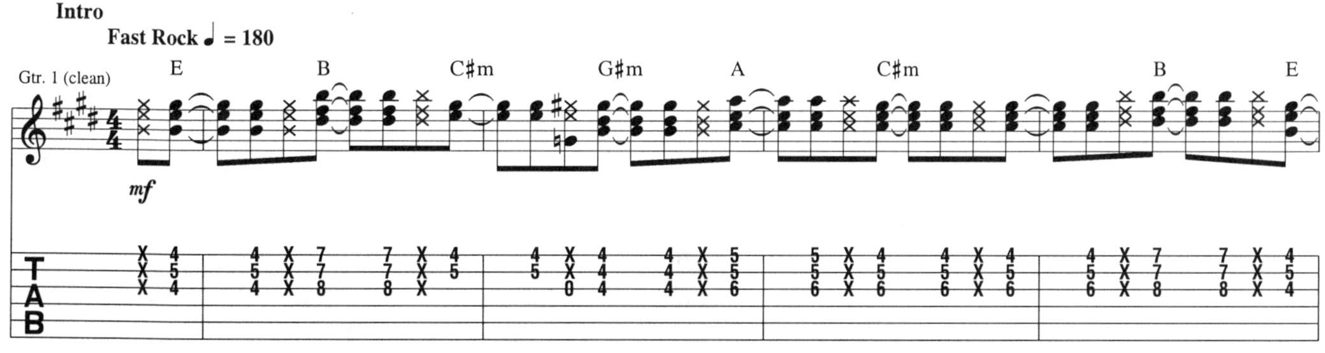

Gtr. 1

B C♯m G♯m A C♯m B

(cont. in slash)

*Gtr. 2

* Horns arr. for gtr.

E B C♯m A E B C♯m A

Rhy. Fig. 1

End Rhy. Fig. 1

Gtr. 1

Gtr. 2

Riff A

Verse

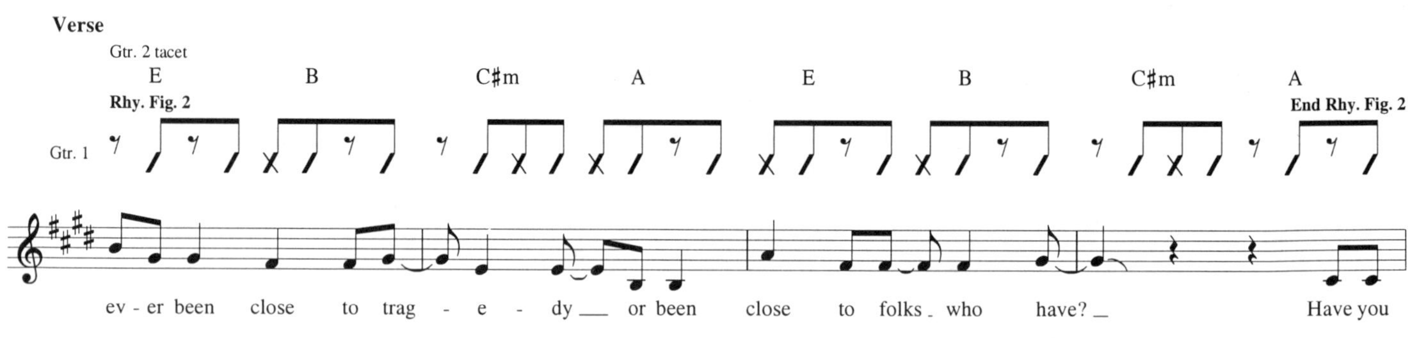

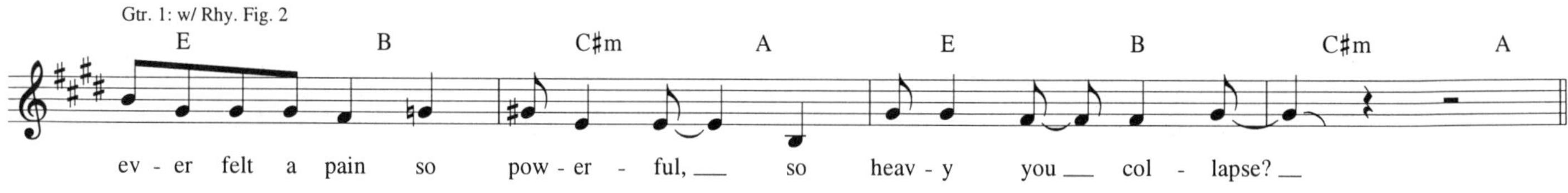

Pre-Chorus

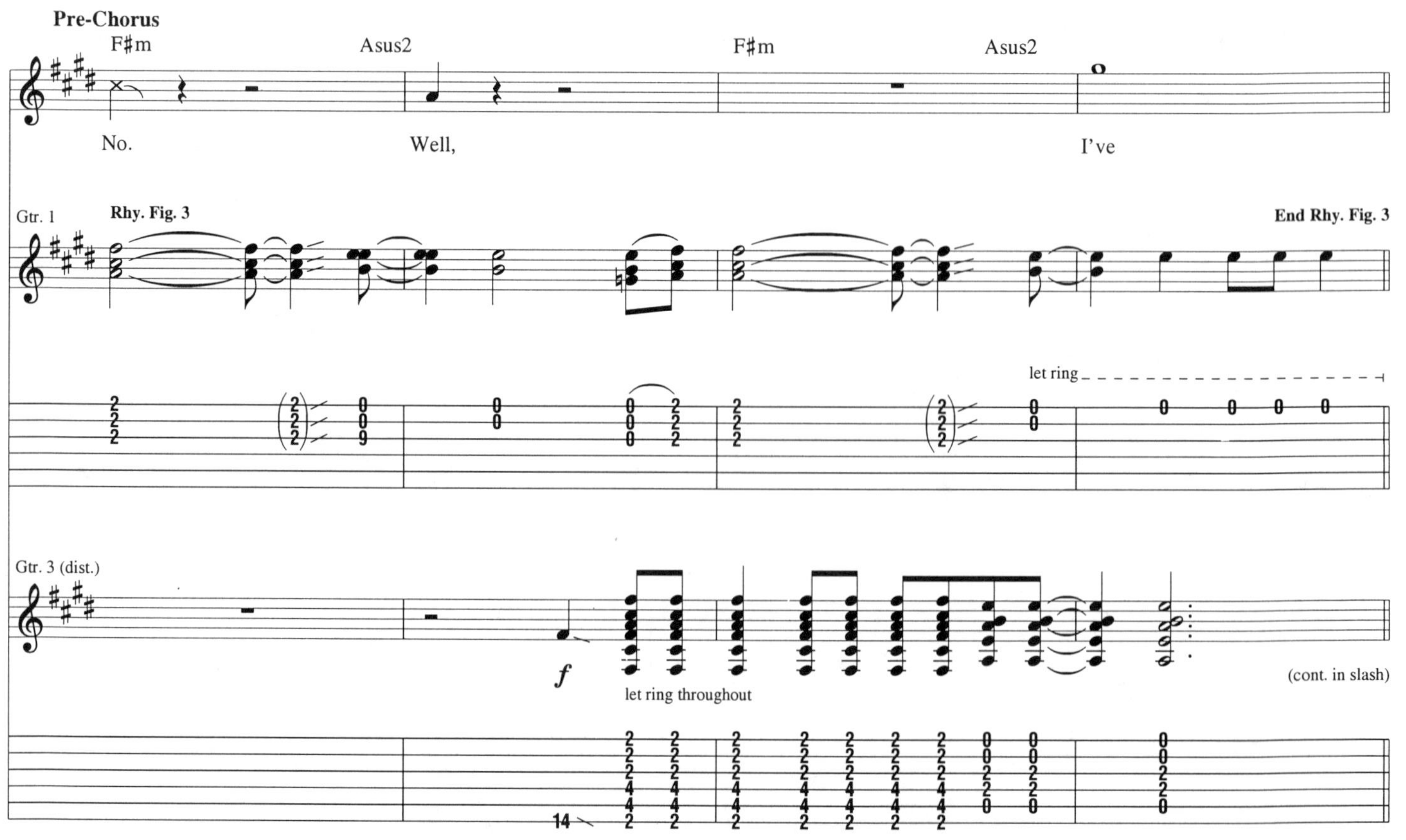

Chorus
E open
B5
G♯5
Rhy. Fig. 4
Gtr. 3
nev - er had to knock on wood, but I know some - one who has,
Gtr. 1
Riff B
*let ring throughout
* next 16 meas.
A5
E open
which makes me won-der if I could. It makes me won-der if I've
B5
nev - er had to knock on wood. And I'm glad I have - n't yet,

G♯5
A5
End Rhy. Fig. 4
because I'm sure it is - n't good. That's the im - pres-sion that I get.
End Riff B
Interlude
Gtr. 1: w/ Rhy. Fig. 1, 2 times, simile
Gtr. 2: w/ Riff A
Gtr. 3 tacet
E B C♯m A E B C♯m A E B C♯m A E B C♯m A
2. Have you
Verse
*E B C♯m A E B C♯m A
ev - er had the odds stacked up so high you need a strength most don't pos - sess? Or has it
Gtr. 1
**slight P.M. throughout
* Chord symbols reflect implied tonality.
** next 8 meas.
E B C♯m A E B
Gtr. 3
P.S.
ev - er come down to do or die? You got to rise a - bove the rest.

Pre-Chorus
Gtr. 1: w/ Rhy. Fig. 3, simile
F♯m
Asus2
Gtr. 3
No. Well, I've
Chorus
Gtrs. 1 & 3: w/ Riff B & Rhy. Fig. 4, simile
E
B5
G♯5
nev - er had to knock on wood,
but I know some - one who has
and I'm glad I have - n't yet
To Coda
A5
which makes me won-der if I could.
be - cause I'm sure it is - n't good.
It makes me won-der if I've
That's the im - pres-sion that I get.
Interlude
F♯m
A5
E
Gtr. 3
Gtr. 1
divisi
Verse
Gtr. 3 tacet
B
C♯m
G♯m
A
3. I'm not a cow-ard, I've just nev-er been test - ed.
I'd like to think that if I was, I would pass.

D.S. al Coda
(take repeat)

B C#m G#m A C#m B

Look at the test-ed and think, there, but for the grace go I. Might be a cow-ard, I'm a - fraid of what I might find out.

Gtr. 1

Gtr. 3

P.S.

Coda

Interlude

Gtr. 1: w/ Rhy. Fig. 1, 2 times, simile
Gtr. 2: w/ Riff A, 1 1/2 times

E B C#m A E B C#m A

Gtr. 1

E B C#m A E B C#m A

*slight P.M. throughout

* next 8 meas.

Outro

Gtrs. 1 & 2 tacet
N.C.(E)
(B)
I've nev - er had to, but I ___ bet - ter knock _ on wood __ 'cause I know some - one __ who has _
(A)
___ which makes me won - der if ___ I could. _ It makes me won - der if ___ I've...
Gtr. 1
p
(E)
(B)
Nev - er had to, but I ___ bet - ter knock _ on wood __ 'cause I'm
pp
(A)
sure it is - n't good ___ and I'm glad I have - n't yet. _
(A)
___ That's the im - pres - sion that __ I get.
decresc.

Loser

Words by Beck Hansen
Music by Beck Hansen and Karl Stephenson
Gtrs. 1 & 3; Drop D Tuning:
①=E ④=D
②=B ⑤=A
③=G ⑥=D
Intro
Moderately Slow Rock
D
G5
play 7 times
D
G5
1. In the
Gtr. 1 (acous.)
Rhy. Fig. 1
End Rhy. Fig. 1
mf w/ slide
Verse
Gtr. 3: w/ Rhy. Fill 1
Gtr. 1 tacet
N.C.(D)
time of chim - pan - zees I was a mon-key, bu-tane in my veins and a mouth to cut the chunk-ies. With the
*Gtr. 2 Riff A
End Riff A
*Sitar arr. for gtr.
Gtr. 2: w/ Riff A, 5 times
plas - tic eye - balls, spray paint the veg - 'ta - bles. Dog food skulls with the beef - cake pan - ty hose.
Gtr. 3: w/ Rhy. Fill 1
Kill the head-lights and put it in neu - tral. Stock car flam-ing with the los - er in the cruise con-trol.
Ba-by's in Re - no with the vi - ta - min D. Got a cou-ple of couch - es, a-sleep on the love - seat.
Rhy. Fill 1
Gtr. 3 (elec.)
mf w/ tremolo & clean tone

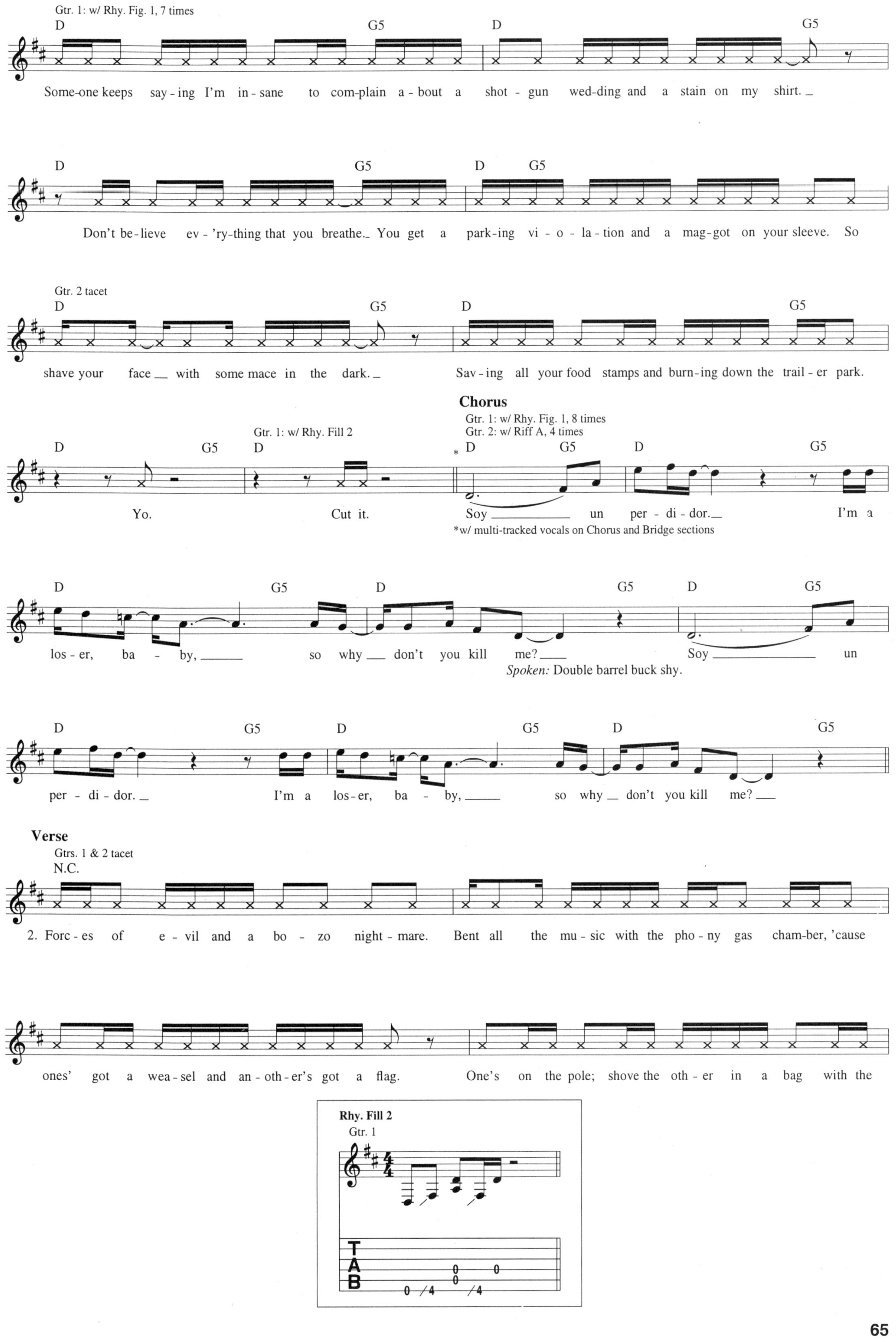

Gtr. 1: w/ Rhy. Fig. 1, 7 times

D G5 D G5

Some-one keeps say - ing I'm in - sane to com-plain a - bout a shot - gun wed-ding and a stain on my shirt. _

D G5 D G5

Don't be-lieve ev - 'ry-thing that you breathe._ You get a park-ing vi - o - la - tion and a mag-got on your sleeve. So

Gtr. 2 tacet

D G5 D G5

shave your face _ with some mace in the dark. _ Sav - ing all your food stamps and burn-ing down the trail - er park.

Gtr. 1: w/ Rhy. Fill 2

D G5 D

Yo. Cut it.

Chorus

Gtr. 1: w/ Rhy. Fig. 1, 8 times
Gtr. 2: w/ Riff A, 4 times

*D G5 D G5

Soy _ un per - di - dor._ I'm a

*w/ multi-tracked vocals on Chorus and Bridge sections

D G5 D G5 D G5
los - er, ba - by, _ so why _ don't you kill me? _ Soy _ un
Spoken: Double barrel buck shy.

D G5 D G5 D G5
per - di - dor. _ I'm a los-er, ba - by, _ so why _ don't you kill me? _

Verse

Gtrs. 1 & 2 tacet
N.C.
2. Forc - es of e - vil and a bo - zo night - mare. Bent all the mu - sic with the pho - ny gas cham-ber, 'cause

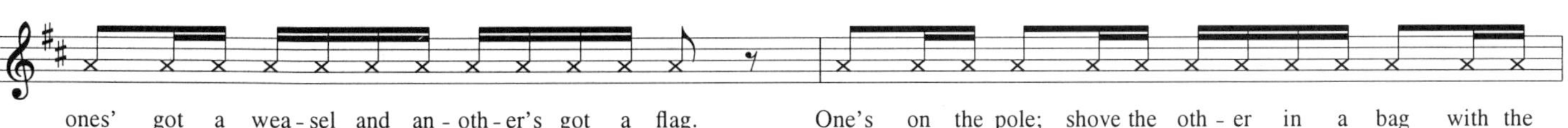
ones' got a wea - sel and an - oth - er's got a flag. One's on the pole; shove the oth - er in a bag with the

Rhy. Fill 2
Gtr. 1
T
A
B

Gtr. 1: w/ Rhy. Fig. 1, 4 times
D G5 D G5
re - run shows _ and the co - caine nose job, the day-time crap of the folk sing - er slob.
D G5 D G5
He hung him-self with a gui - tar string. _ A slab of tur - key neck, and its' hang-ing from a pi - geon wing.
Gtr. 1 tacet
N.C. (D7)
A - get right if you can't re - late. _ Trade the cash for the beef, for the bod - y, for the hate. And my
Gtr. 3
time is a piece of wax _ fall - in' on a ter - mite who's chok - in' on the splin-ters.
Gtr. 3
Chorus
Gtr. 1: w/ Rhy. Fig. 1, 7 times
Gtr. 2: w/ Riff A, 3 1/2 times
Gtr. 3 tacet
D G5 D G5 D G5 D G5
Soy _ un per - di - dor. _ I'm a los-er, ba - by, _ so why _ don't you kill me? _
Spoken: Get crazy with the Cheez Whiz.
Gtr. 1: w/ Rhy. Fill 1
Gtr. 2: w/ Rhy. Fill 3
D G5 D G5 D G5 D G5
Soy _ un per - di - dor. _ I'm a lo-ser, ba - by, _ so why _ don't you kill me? _
Spoken: Drive-by body pierce.
Rhy. Fill 3
Gtr. 2

Bridge
Gtrs. 1 & 2 tacet
N.C.
Yo, bring it on down. Soy.
Gtr. 1: w/ Rhy. Fig. 1, 7 times
w/ Bkgd. voc. ad Lib, next 4 meas.
D G5 D G5 D G5 D G5
Soy.
Gtr. 3
Gtr. 2: w/ Riff A, 1 1/2 times
Gtr. 1: w/ Rhy. Fill 4
Gtr. 2: w/ Rhy. Fill 5
Spoken: I'm a driver, I'm a winner. Things are gonna change. I can feel it.
Chorus
4th time, Begin Fade
Gtr. 1: w/ Rhy. Fig. 1, 4 times
Gtr. 2: w/ Riff A, 2 times
Gtr. 3 tacet
So, un per - di - dor. I'm a los-er, ba - by, so why don't you kill me?
Spoken: I can't believe it.
Outro
Gtr. 3: w/ Rhy. Fill 1
Gtr. 2: w/ Riff A, till fade
Gtr. 1 tacet
Repeat and Fade
N.C. (D)
don't you kill me? don't you kill me? don't you kill me?
Spoken: Uuuuuuuuuuh. Spoken: Sprechen Sie Deutsch, baby? Spoken: You know what I'm sayin'?
Rhy. Fill 4
Gtr. 1
Rhy. Fill 5
Gtr. 2

Man in the Box

Lyrics by Layne Staley
Music by Jerry Cantrell

Ah ah, ah, ah, ah, ah,
ah, ah, ah.
Verse
1. I'm the man in the box.
2. I'm the dog who gets beat.
Guitar 2 out
Guitar 1 (with talk box set to open on heavy accents)
Bur - ied in my shit.
Shove my nose in shit.

Pre - chorus
Won't
you
envelope filter off
SL
P.M.
come
and
save
me?
talk box on
vib.
P.M.
Save
me.
Fill 1 on 2nd verse
Fill 1
8va
instead of guitar lick from 1st verse
1/2
1/2

E5
G5
D
A5
Chorus
Feed
my
eyes,
Bkgd. (can
you sew
them
shut?
)
1/4
E5
G5
D/A
Je
-
sus
Christ,
A5
E5
G5
(De
-
ny
your ma
-
ker
)
He
D/A
A5
who
tries.
Ah,
(Will
be wast
-
ed.
)

E5
G5
D/A
feed
my
eyes,
A5
2nd time vocals out
To Coda
(Now
you've
sewn
them
shut.)
Guitar Solo
Guitar 2
with wah-wah
full
full
full

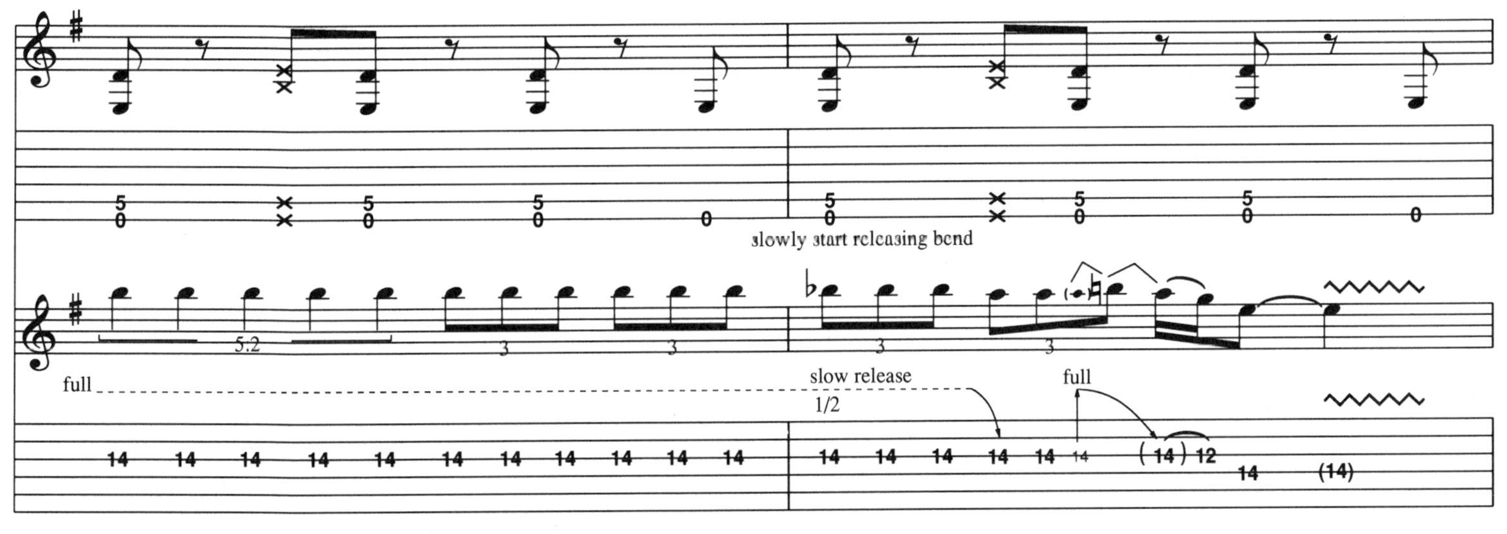
slowly start releasing bend
full
slow release
1/2
full

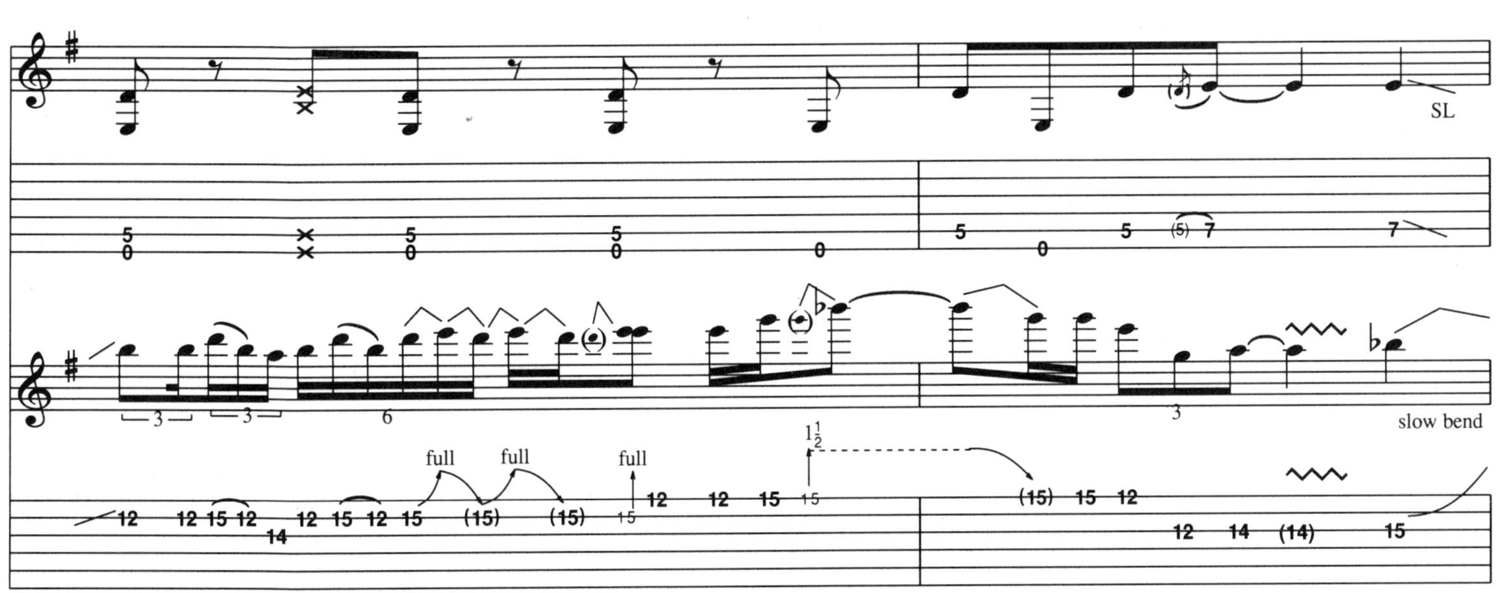
SL
full
full
full
slow bend

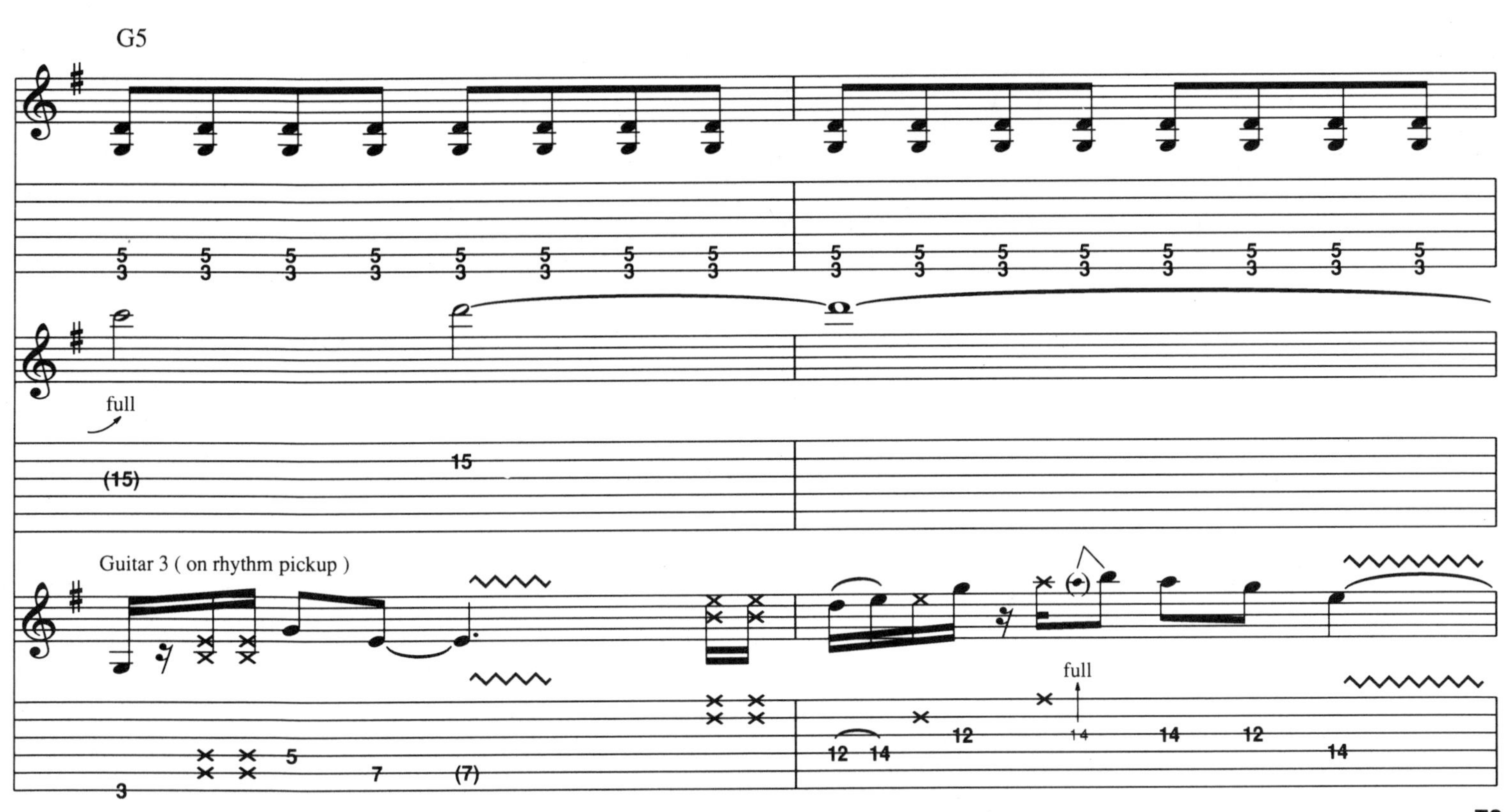
G5
full
Guitar 3 (on rhythm pickup)
full

(with talk box on accents)

8va
loco
Guitar 2

catches feedback

A.H.

1/2

Guitar 3 out

1/2

1/2

talk box off

D. S. al Coda

(on rhythm pick up)

semi -A.H. 1/4

Guitar 3

full

full

Coda

Ah, ah, ah, ah, ah, ah,
(Guitar 1 continues rhythm fig. 1 two more times)
Guitar 2 (Guitar with wah-wah)
ah, ah, ah.
Ah, ah, ah, ah, ah, ah,
ah, ah, ah.

The Man Who Sold The World

Words and Music by David Bowie

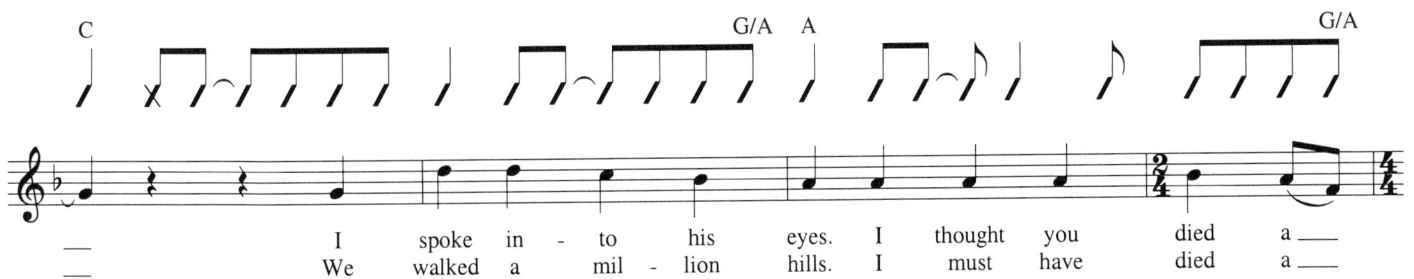
C
G/A
A
G/A
I spoke in - to his eyes. I thought you died a
We walked a mil - lion hills. I must have died a

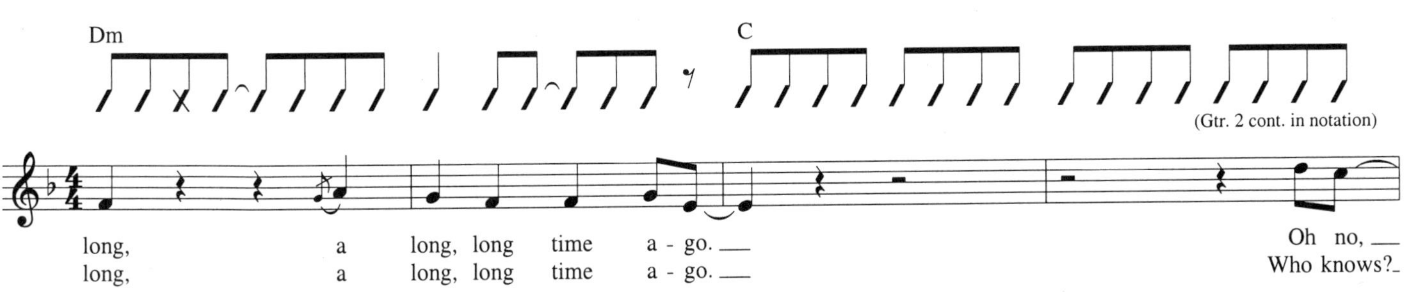
Dm
C
(Gtr. 2 cont. in notation)
long, a long, long time a - go.
long, a long, long time a - go.
Oh no,
Who knows?

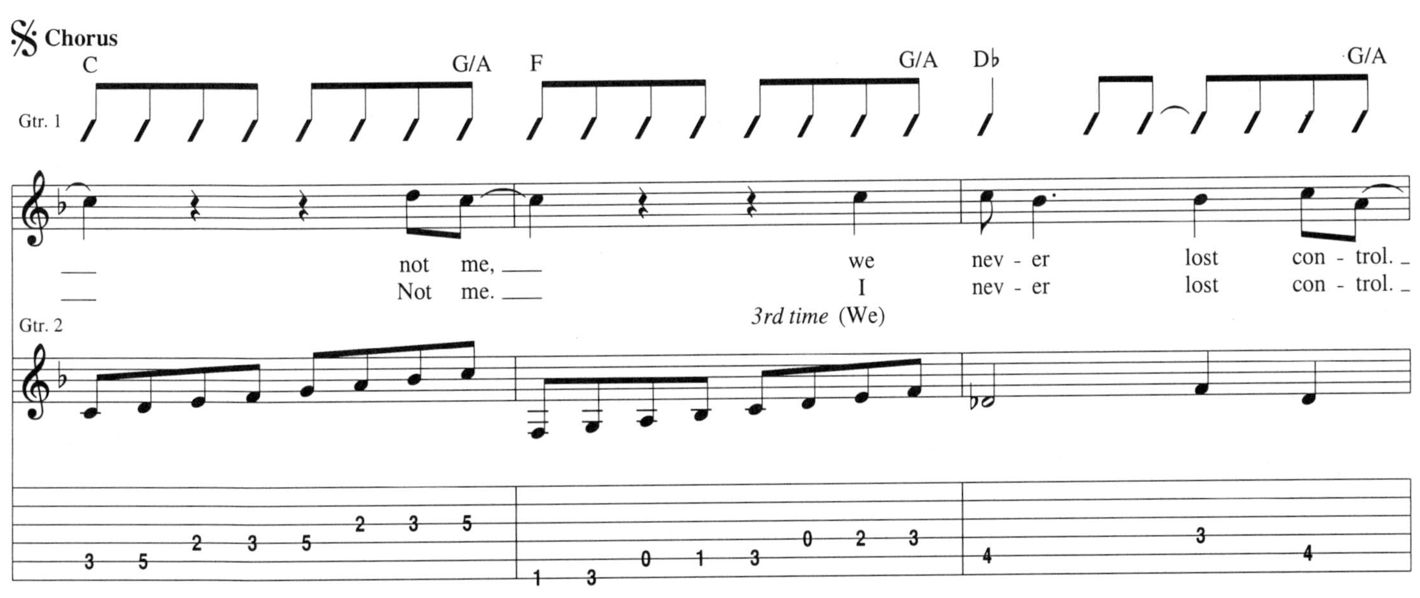
Chorus
C
G/A
F
G/A
D♭
G/A
Gtr. 1
not me, we nev - er lost con - trol.
Not me. I nev - er lost con - trol.
3rd time (We)
Gtr. 2

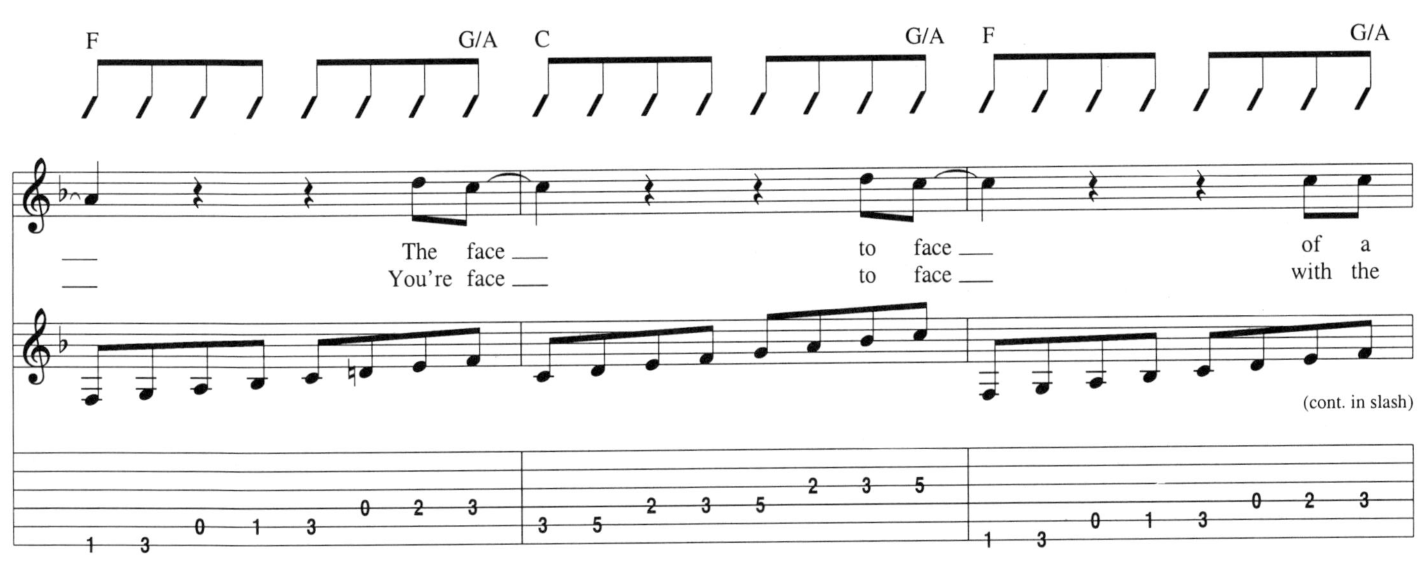
F
G/A
C
G/A
F
G/A
The face to face of a
You're face to face with the
(cont. in slash)

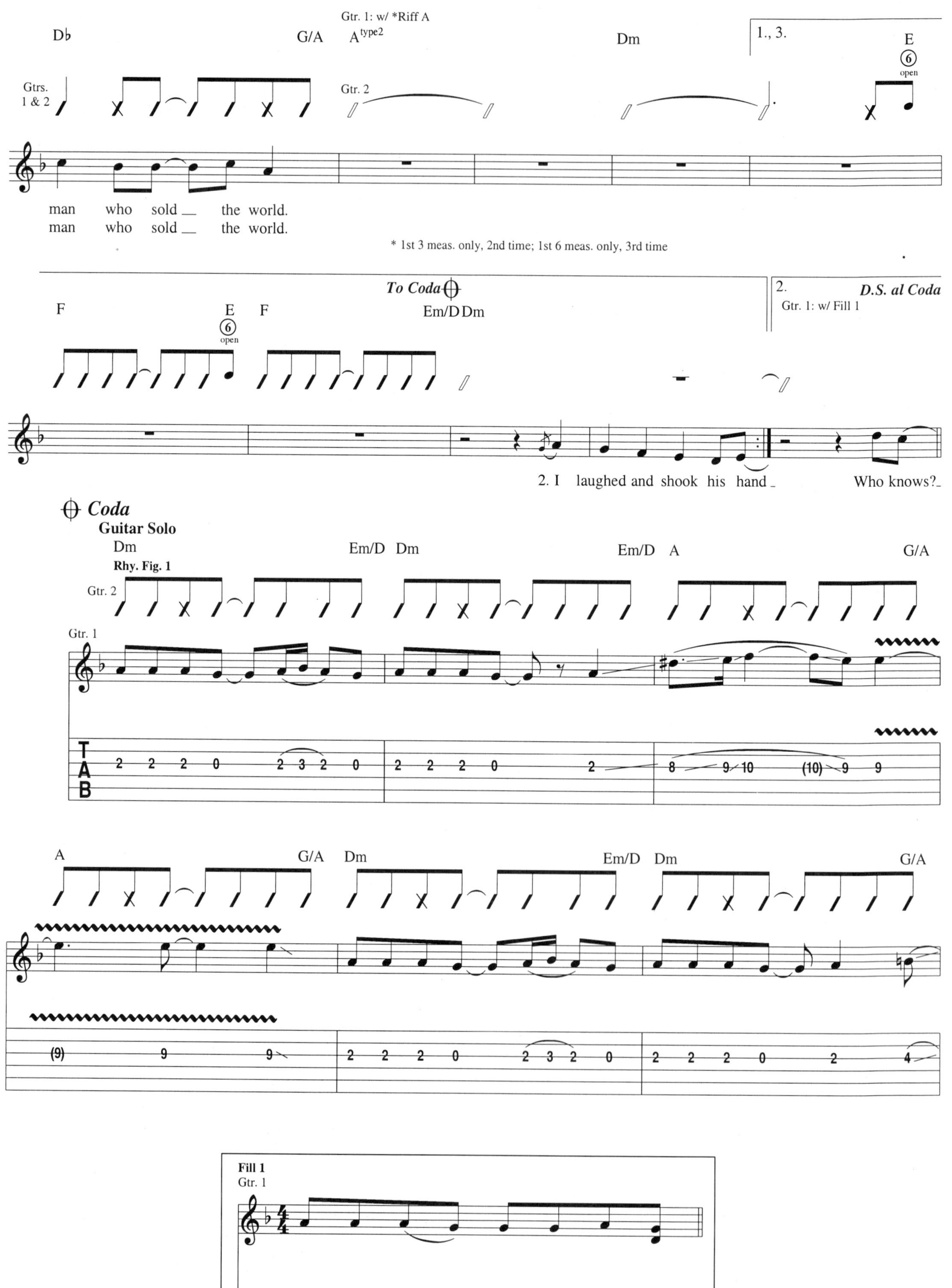
Gtr. 1: w/ *Riff A
D♭
G/A
A type2
Dm
1., 3.
E
open
Gtrs. 1 & 2
Gtr. 2
man who sold __ the world.
man who sold __ the world.
* 1st 3 meas. only, 2nd time; 1st 6 meas. only, 3rd time
To Coda
2.
D.S. al Coda
Gtr. 1: w/ Fill 1
F
E
F
Em/D Dm
2. I laughed and shook his hand _ Who knows?_
Coda
Guitar Solo
Dm
Em/D Dm
Em/D A
G/A
Rhy. Fig. 1
Gtr. 2
Gtr. 1
A
G/A
Dm
Em/D
Dm
G/A
Fill 1
Gtr. 1

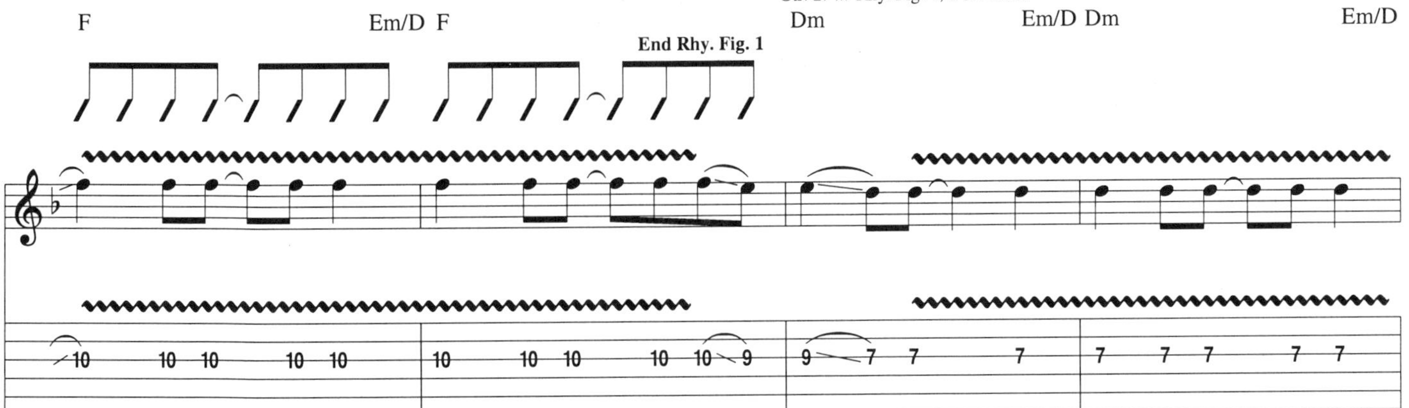
Gtr. 2: w/ Rhy. Fig. 1, 1 3/4 times
F
Em/D F
End Rhy. Fig. 1
Dm
Em/D Dm
Em/D

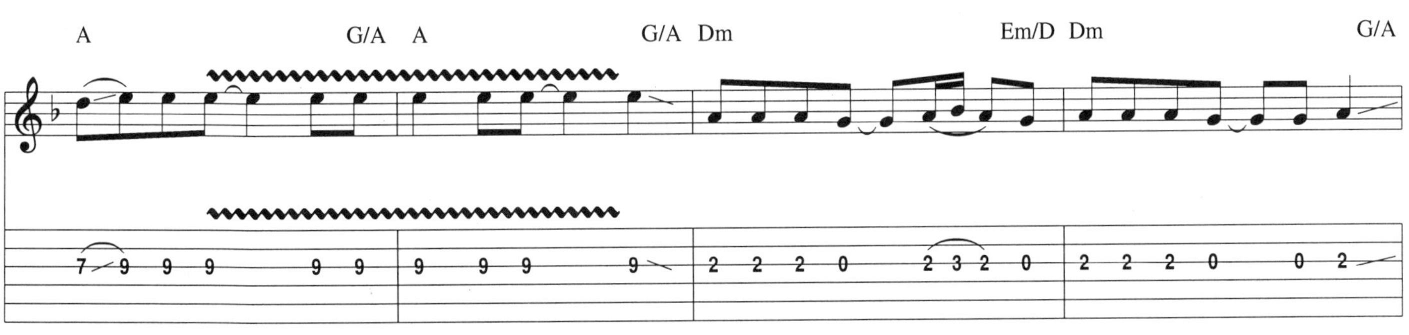
A
G/A A
G/A Dm
Em/D Dm
G/A

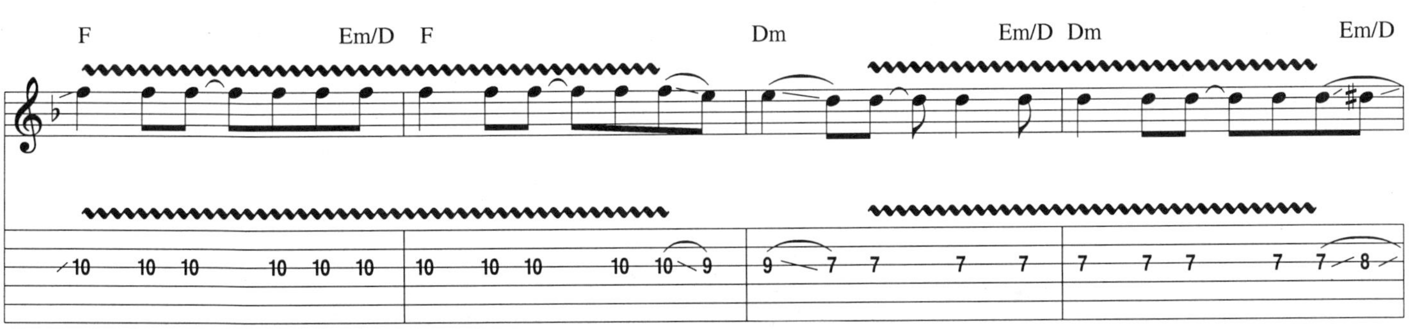
F
Em/D F
Dm
Em/D Dm
Em/D

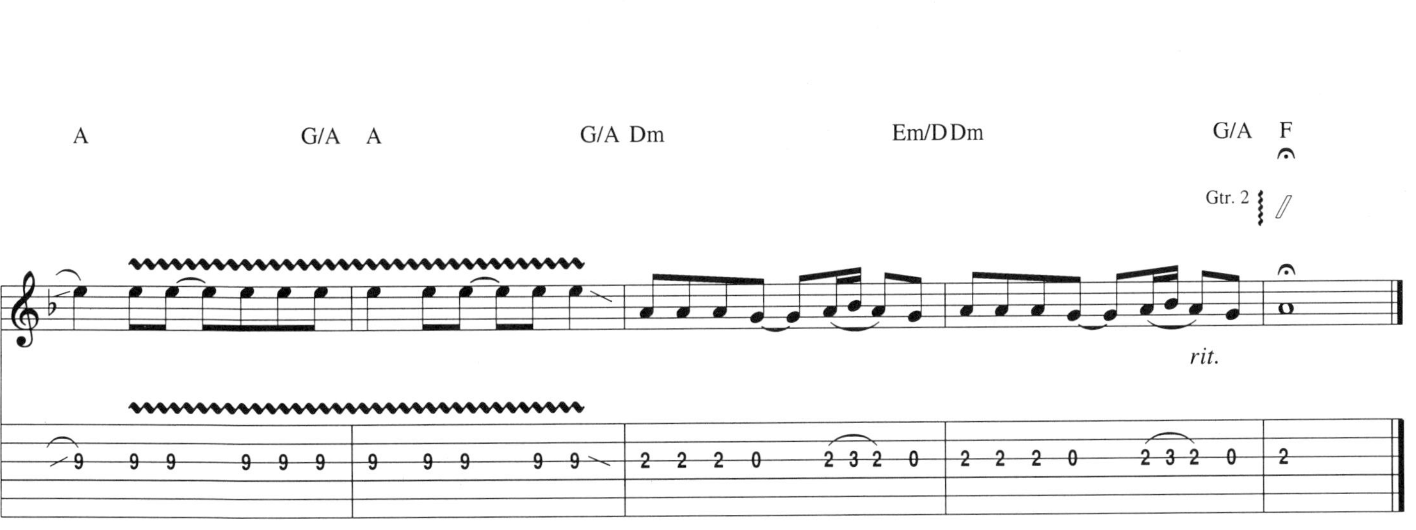
A
G/A A
G/A Dm
Em/D Dm
G/A F
Gtr. 2
rit.

Self Esteem

Words and Music by Dexter Holland

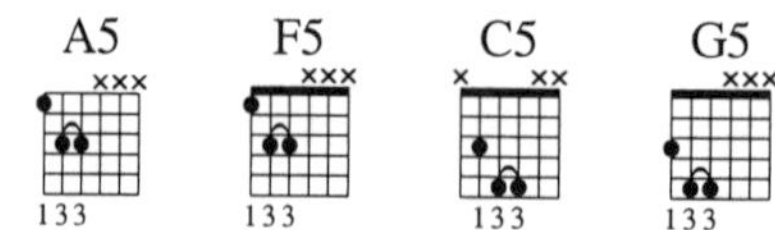

*Two gtrs. arr. for one.

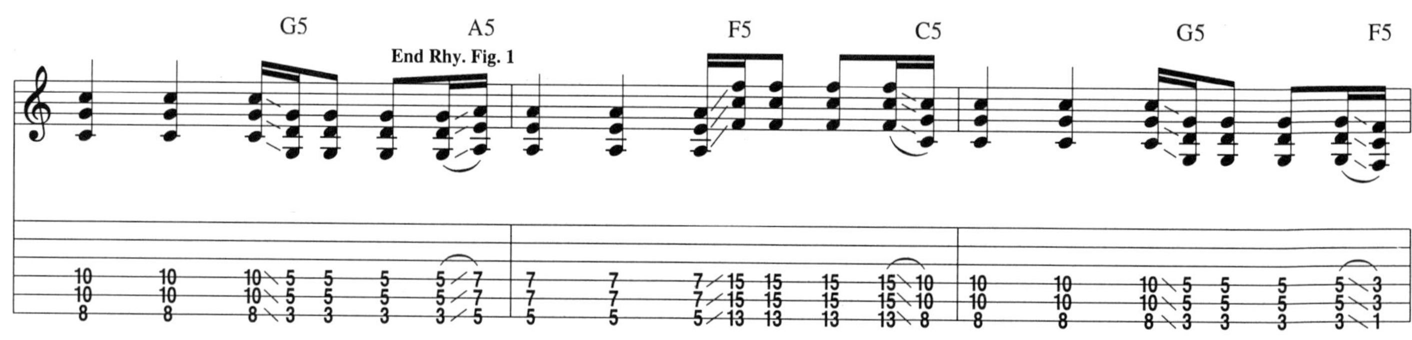

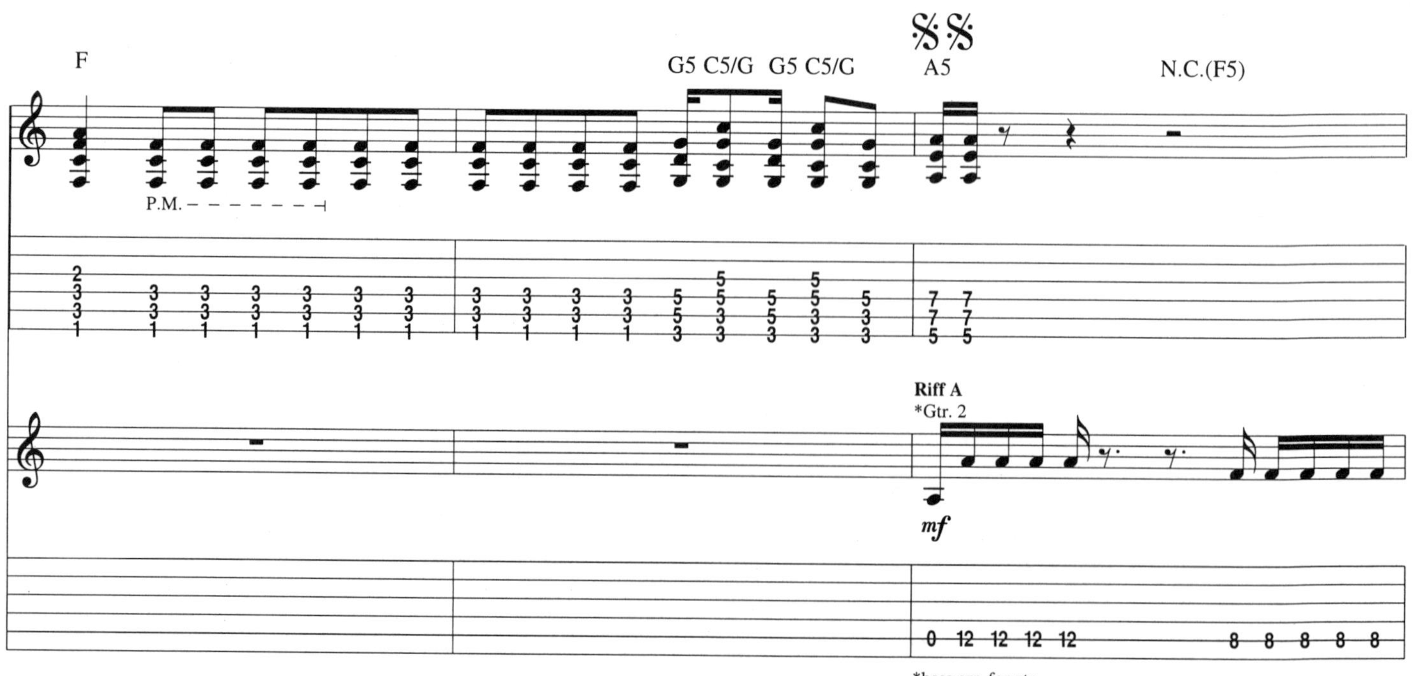

*bass arr. for gtr.

(C5) (G5) (A5) (F5) (C5) G5
End Riff A
Verse
Gtr. 1 tacet
Gtr. 2: w/ Riff A, 8 times
N.C.(A5) (F5) (C5) (G5) (A5) (F5) (C5) (G5)
1. I wrote her off for the tenth time to - day (and) prac-ticed all the things I would say.
3. Now I'll re - late this lit - tle bit that hap-pens more than I'd like to ad - mit.
(A5) (F5) (C5) (G5) (A5) (F5) (C5) G5
But she came o - ver, I lost my nerve. I took her back and made her des - sert.
Late at night she knocks on my door. She's drunk a - gain and look-ing to score.
Gtr. 1
(cont. in slash)
Pre-Chorus
G5 A5 F5 C5 G5 A5 F5
Gtr. 1
P.M.
(Now) I know I'm be - in' used. That's o - kay man 'cause I
(Now) I know I should say no, but that's kind of hard when she's
C5 G5 A5 F5 C5 G5
Rhy. Fig. 2
like the a - buse. I know she's play - ing with me.
read - y to go. I may be dumb but I'm not a dweeb.
Chorus
Gtr. 2 tacet
Gtr. 1: w/ Rhy. Fig. 1, 4 times
A5 F5 C5 G5 A5 F5 C5
End Rhy. Fig. 2
* P.M.
That's o - kay 'cause I've got no self es - teem.
I'm just a suck - er with no self es - teem.
Oh, hey, yeah, ay, yeah.
* gradually less P.M.

G5 A5 F5 C5 G5 A5 F5 C5 G5 A5
Yeah. Oh, yeah, yeah. Oh, yeah. Yeah.
To Coda
Verse
Gtr. 1 tacet
Gtr. 2: w/ Riff A, 4 times
F5 C5 G5 A5 N.C.(A5) (F5) (C5) (G5) (A5) (F5)
Oh, yeah, yeah. 2. We make plans to go out at night. I wait till two then I
Gtr. 1: w/ Rhy. Fig. 2
D.S. al Coda
G5 A5 F5 C5 G5 A5 F5 C5 G5
Gtr. 1
P.M.
turn out the light. This re-jec-tion's got me so low. (If)she keeps it up, I just might tell her so. Oh,
Coda
Bridge
D5 B♭5 F5 C5 D5 B♭5
When she's say - ing ah, that she wants on - ly me. Then I won - der why she
When she's say - ing oh, that I'm like a dis - ease. Then I won - der how much
Well I guess I should stick up for my - self, but I real - ly think it's
Gtr. 1
F5 C5 D5 B♭5 C5 G5 F5
play 3 times
sleeps with my friends. The more you suf - fer, the more it shows you real - ly
more I can spend.
bet - ter this way.
1.
D.S.S. al Coda
2.
G5 C5/G G5 C5/G F5 G5 C5/G G5 C5/G A5
care. Right? Yeah. Right? Yeah.
P.M.

Silent Lucidity

Words and Music by Chris DeGarmo

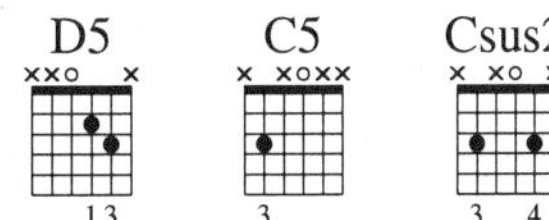

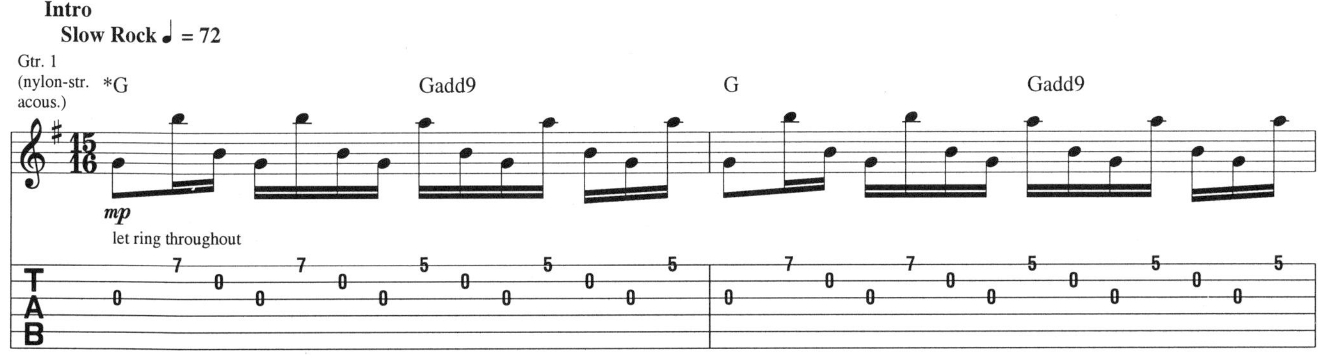

* Chord symbols reflect implied tonality.

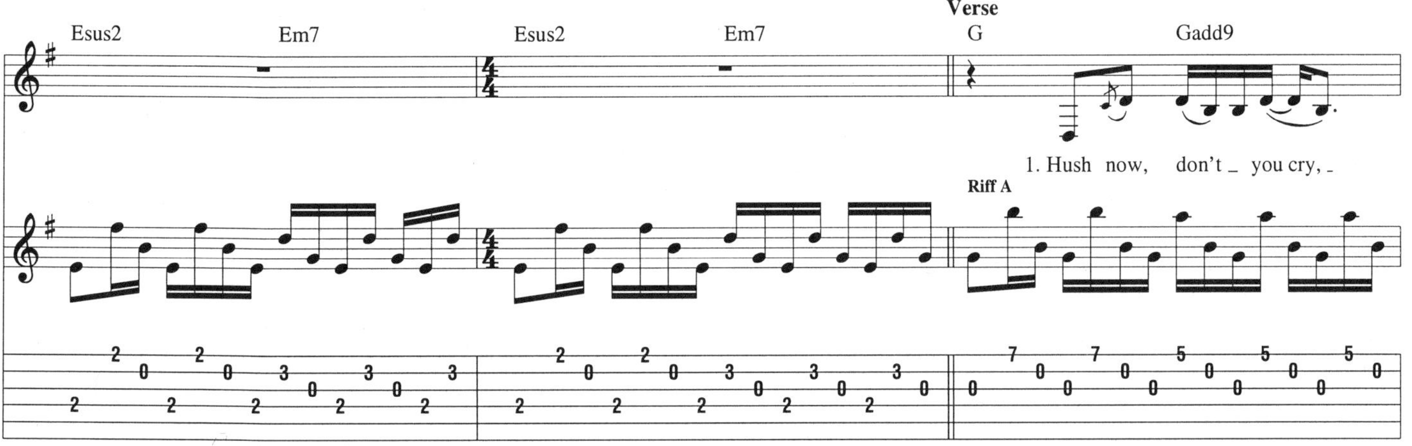

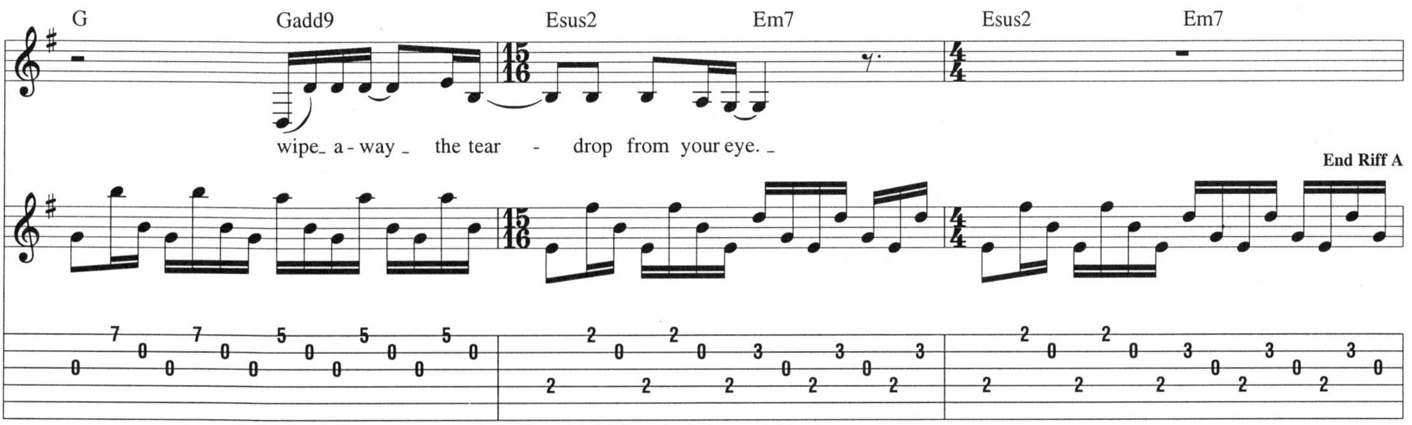

Esus2 Em7 C Csus2 C Csus2
Your mind tricked you to feel the pain of some - one close to you
Riff B
Gtr. 1
Am7 A7sus4 Am7 A7sus4
leav - ing the game of life.
End Riff B
Gtr. 1: w/ Riff B, 1st 3 meas.
C Csus2 C Csus2 Am7 A7sus4
So here it is, an - oth - er chance, wide a - wake you face the day, your dream is o - ver...
Interlude
G Gsus2
or has it just be - gun?
Gtr. 1
Gtr. 2
(12-str. acous.)
divisi
mf
Gtrs. 1 & 2
let ring throughout
G Gsus2 Esus2 Em7 Esus2 Em7

Verse
Gtr. 4: w/ Fill 1, 2nd time
Gtr. 5 tacet, 2nd time
G
Gsus2
G
Gsus2
2. There's a place I like to hide, a door - way that I
3. If you o - pen your mind for me, you won't re - ly on
Riff C
Esus2
Em7
Esus2
Em7
run through in the night.
o - pen eyes to see.
End Riff C
Gtrs. 1 & 2: w/ Riff C
G
Gsus2
G
Gsus2
Esus2
Em7
Re - lax, child, you were there, but on - ly did - n't re - al - ize (it), and you were scared.
The walls you built with - in, come tumb - ling down and a new world will be - gin.
Esus2
Em7
Gtrs. 1 & 2: w/ Riff B, 1 3/4 times
C
Csus2
C
Csus2
It's a place where you will learn to face your fears, re -
Liv - ing twice at once, you learn you're safe from pain in the
Am7
A7sus4
Am7
A7sus4
C
Csus2
trace the years and ride the whims of your mind. Com - mand - ing in an - oth - er world,
dream do - main. A soul set free to fly. A round - trip jour - ney in your head,
C
Csus2
Am7
A7sus4
sud - den - ly, you hear and see this mag - ic new di - men -
mas - ter of il - lus - sion, can you re - al - ize your
Fill 1
Gtr. 4
TAB
(4)

Chorus
Gtrs. 1 & 2 tacet
Am7
A7
D5
Gtr. 4 (elec.)
mf w/ dist.
- sion.
dream's a - live, you can be the guide but... (I
Gtrs. 1 & 2
Gtr. 3 (elec.)
f
w/ clean tone
let ring throughout
C5
D5
...will be watch - ing o - ver you.
I...
C5
D5
...am gon - na help to see it through.
I...
C5
D5
...will pro - tect you in the night.
I...
End Riff D

To Coda

Csus2

am smil - ing next to you, ___ in si - lent lu - cid - i - ty. ___

Gtr. 1

Gtr. 3
divisi

Guitar Solo

Gtr. 1: w/ Riff A, 1st 2 meas.
Gtrs. 3 & 4 tacet

G Gadd9 G Gadd9

Gtr. 1 tacet

E♭ E♭sus2

Gtr. 4

f

full

1 1/2

Gtr. 2

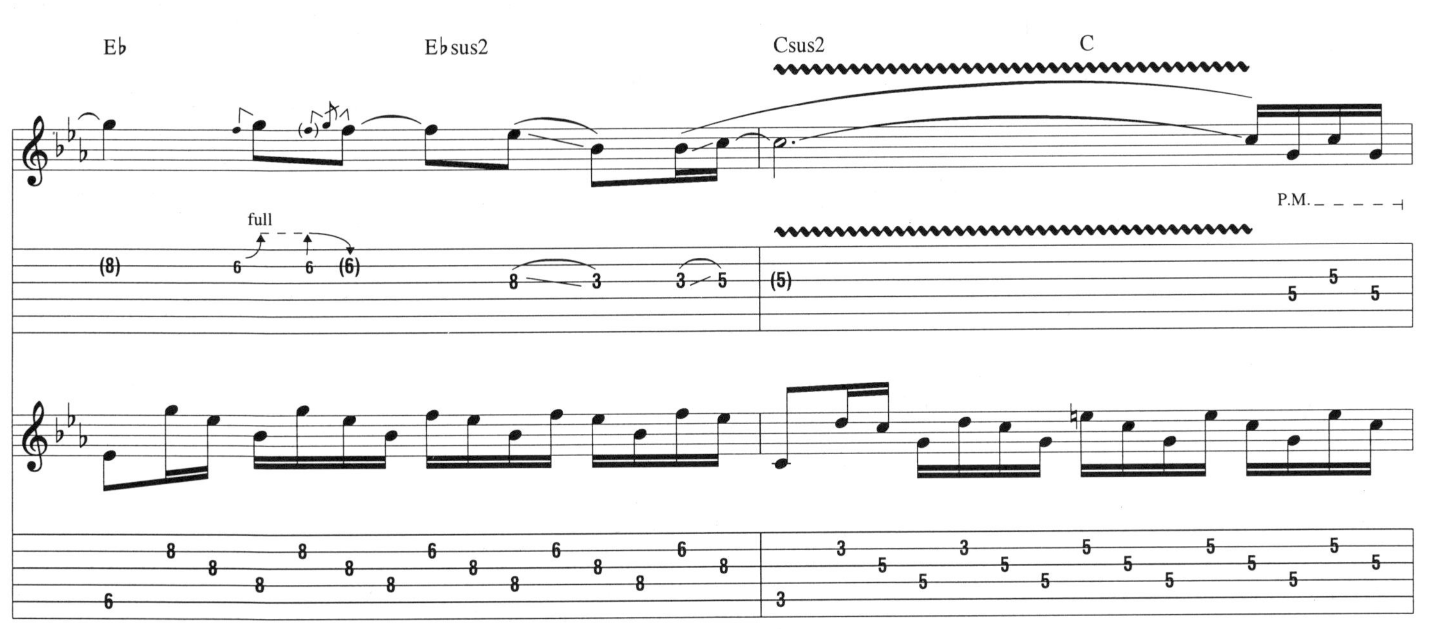

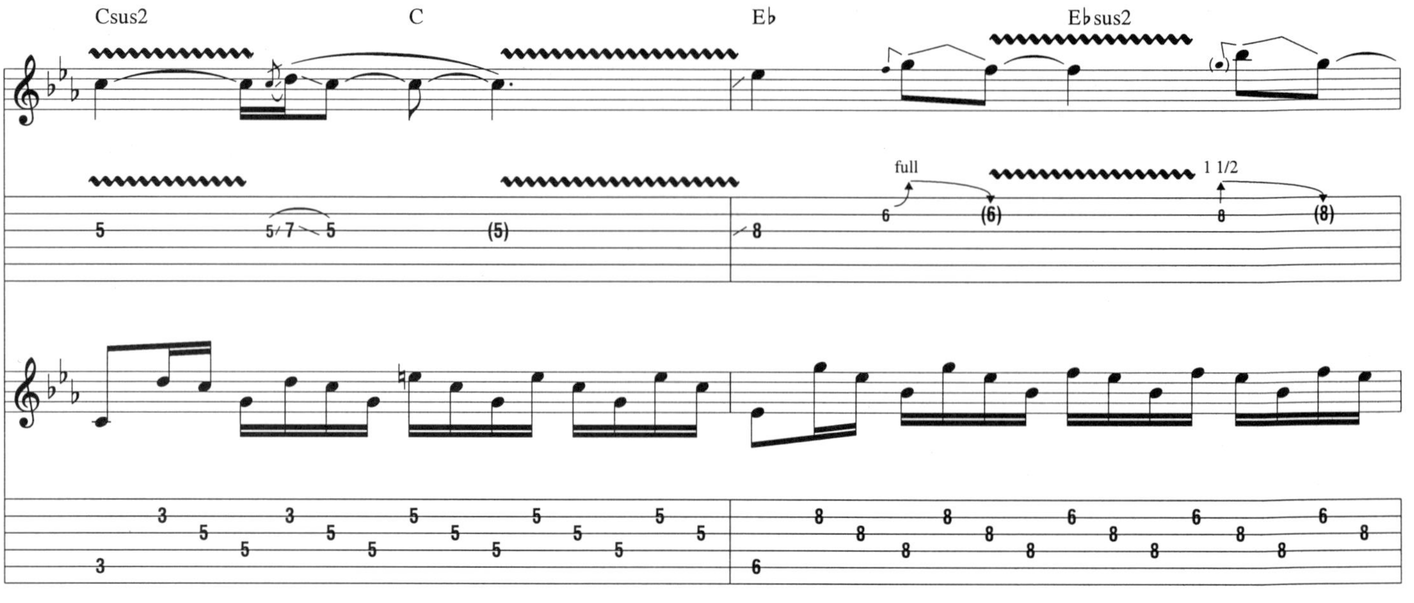

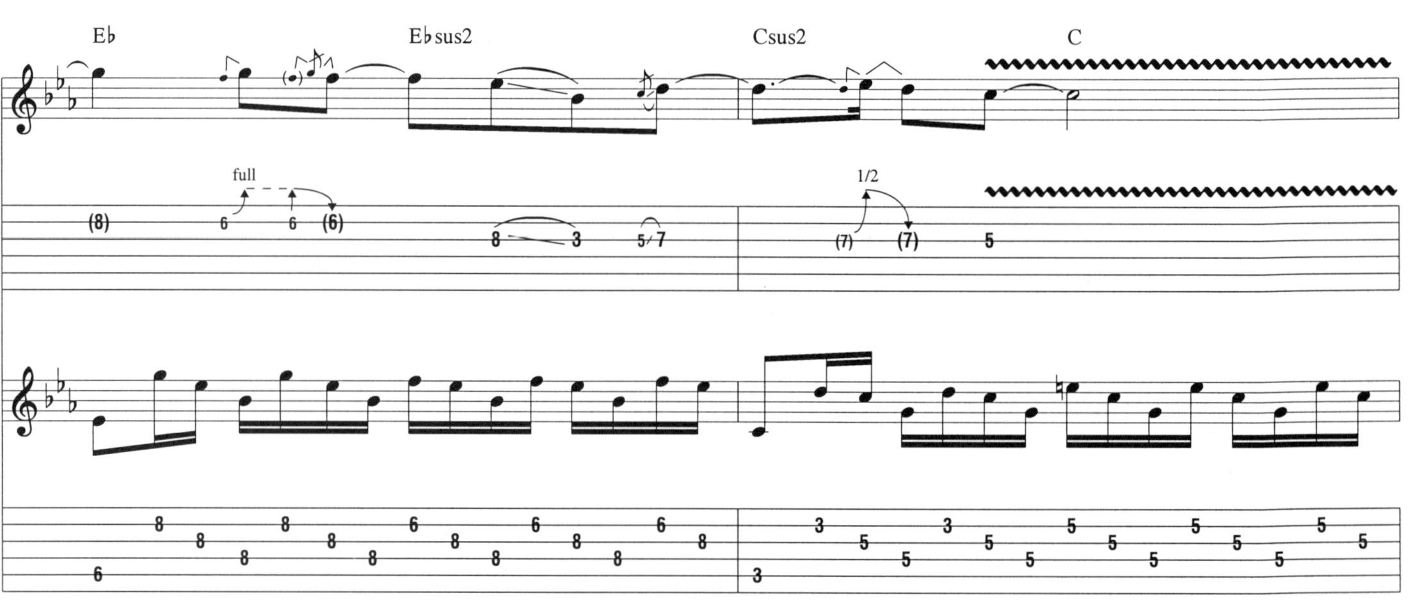

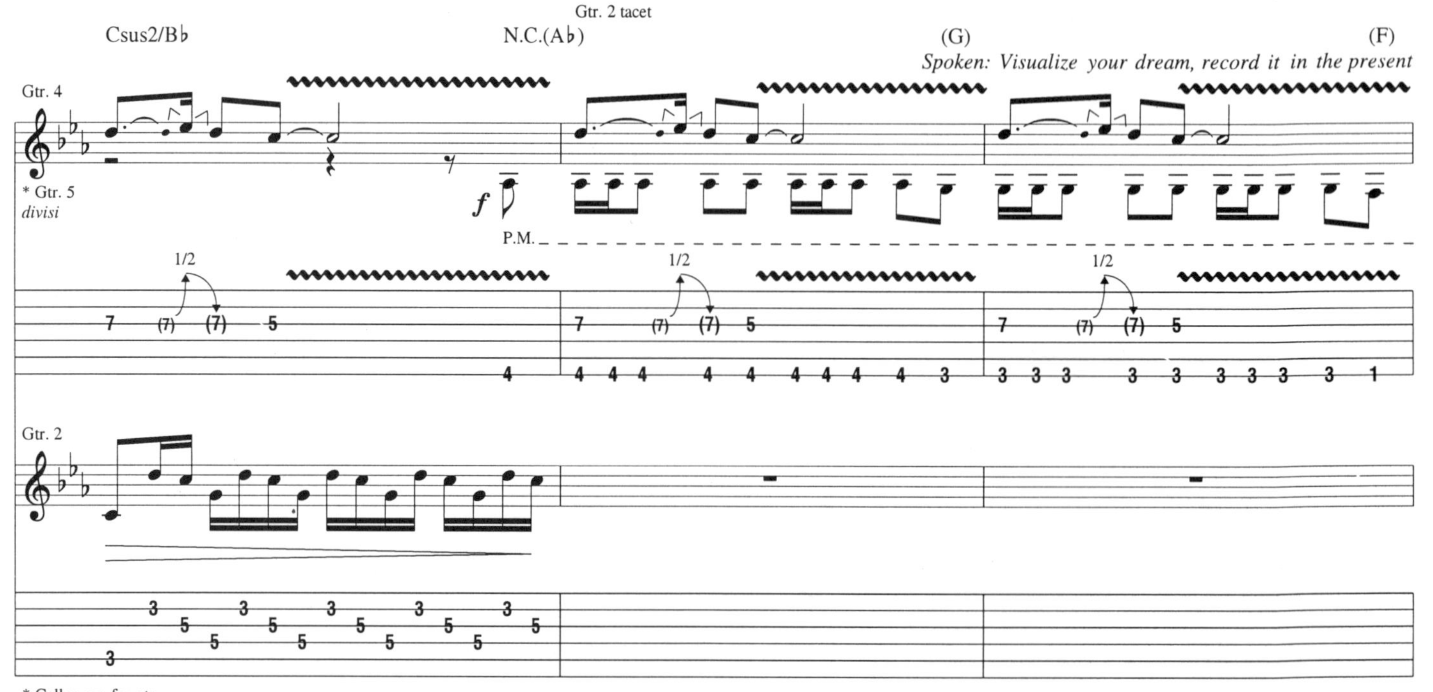

* Cellos arr. for gtr.

(E♭)
tense, put it into a permanent form. If you persist in your efforts, you can achieve dream control...
(D)
control...
(C)
P.M.
1/2
D.S. al Coda
dream control . . .
(B♭)
dream control... dream control . . .
(A♭)
(G)
dream control.
Coda
Outro
Gtrs. 3 & 4 tacet
G
Gadd9
Gtr. 1
Gtr. 5 (nylon-str. acous.)
p

Spiderwebs

Words and Music by Gwen Stefani and Tony Kanal

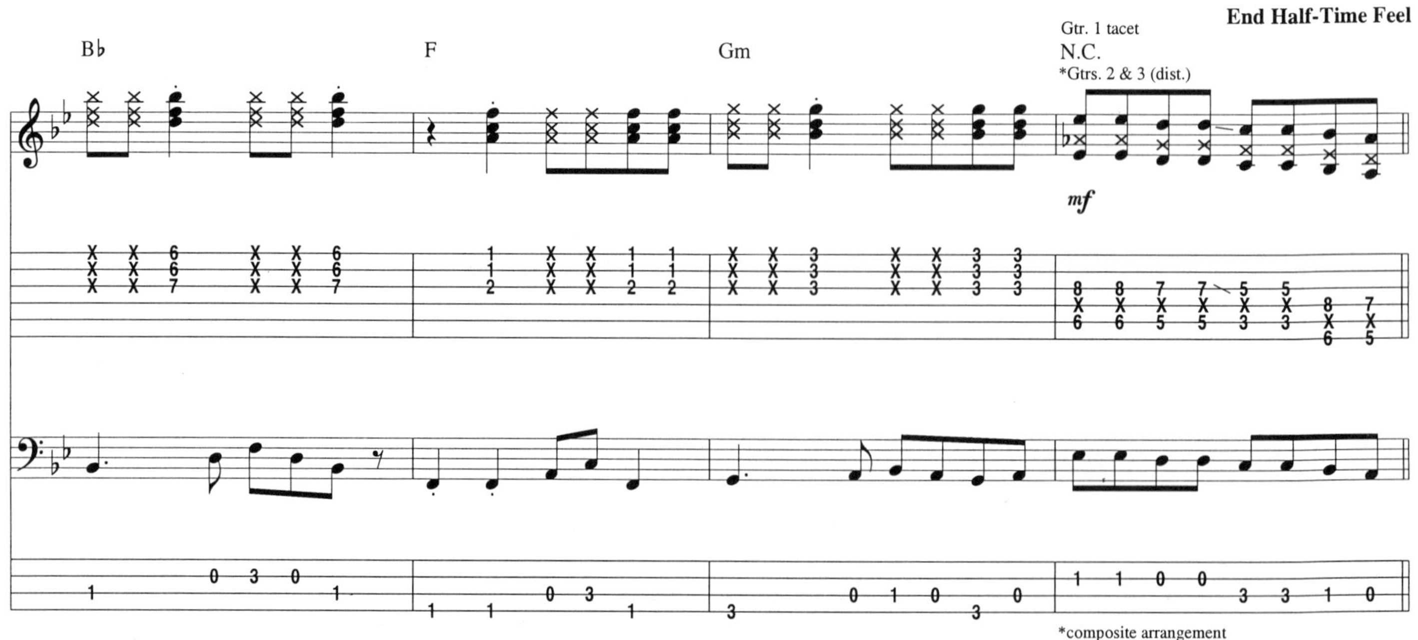

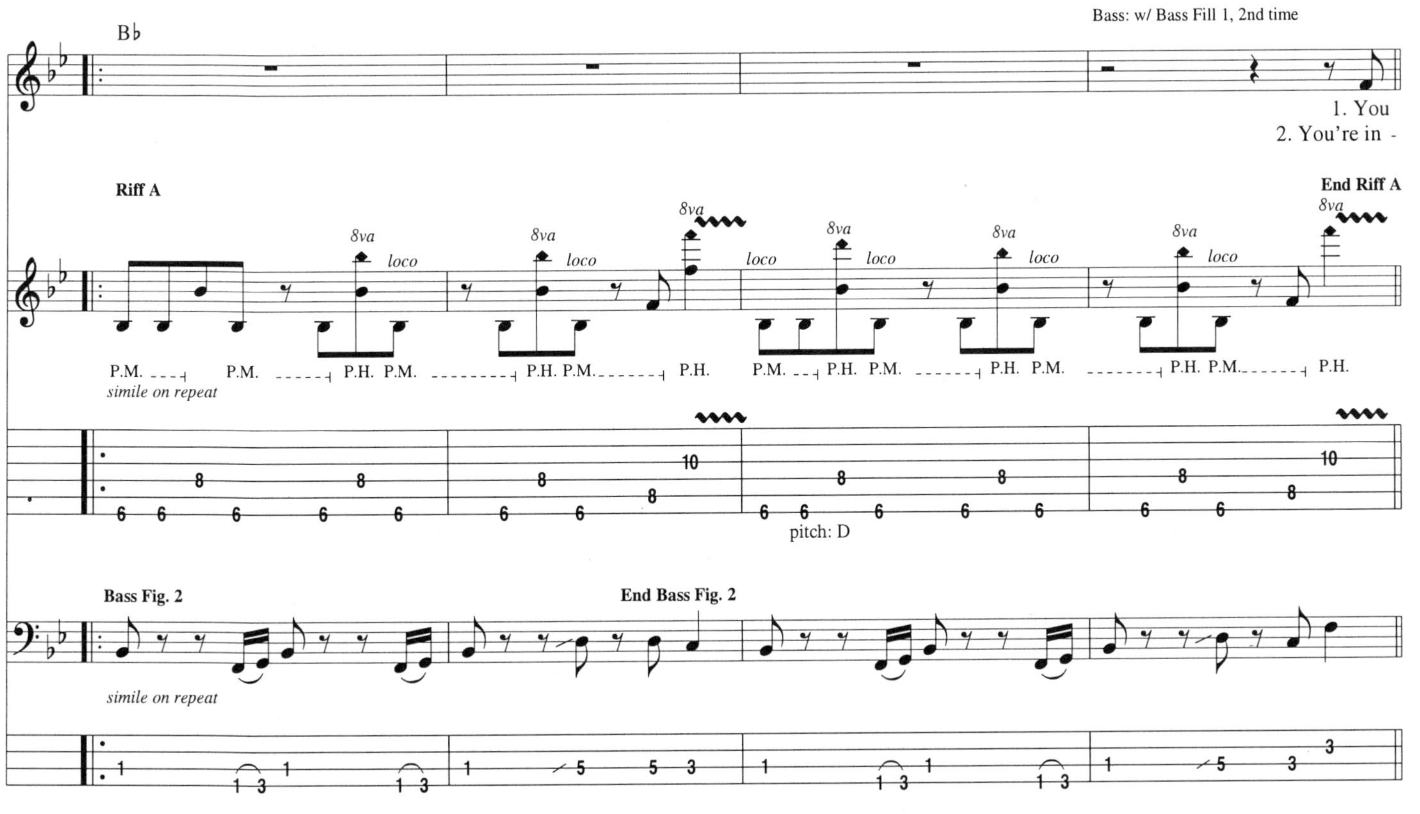
Bass: w/ Bass Fill 1, 2nd time
B♭
1. You
2. You're in -
Riff A
End Riff A
8va
loco
P.M.
P.H.
simile on repeat
pitch: D
Bass Fig. 2
End Bass Fig. 2

Verse

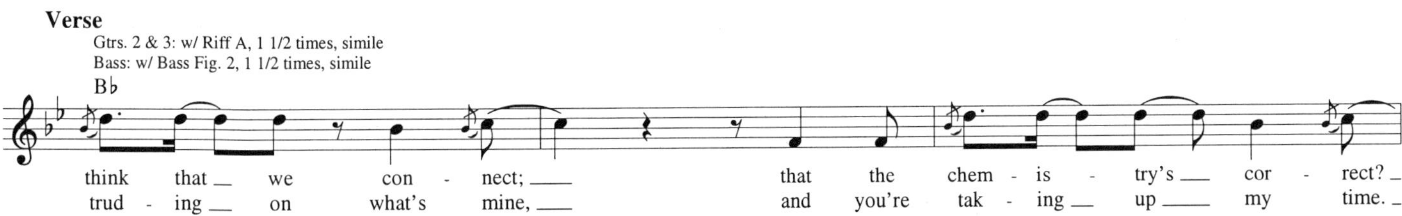
Gtrs. 2 & 3: w/ Riff A, 1 1/2 times, simile
Bass: w/ Bass Fig. 2, 1 1/2 times, simile
B♭
think that we con - nect; that the chem - is - try's cor - rect?
trud - ing on what's mine, and you're tak - ing up my time.

Bass: w/ Bass Fill 2, 2nd time
Your words walk right through my ears, pre - sum - ing
Don't have the cour - age in - side me to tell you,
Bass

Bass Fill 1
Bass

Bass Fill 2
Bass

Pre-Chorus

N.C.

E♭5

Gtr. 3

I like what I hear. And now I'm
"Please (just) let me be." Com - mu - ni -

Gtrs. 2 & 3

8va

loco

Gtr. 2

P.M. P.H. P.M.

(Gtr. 3 cont. in slash)

P.M.

pitch: D

Bass

simile on repeat

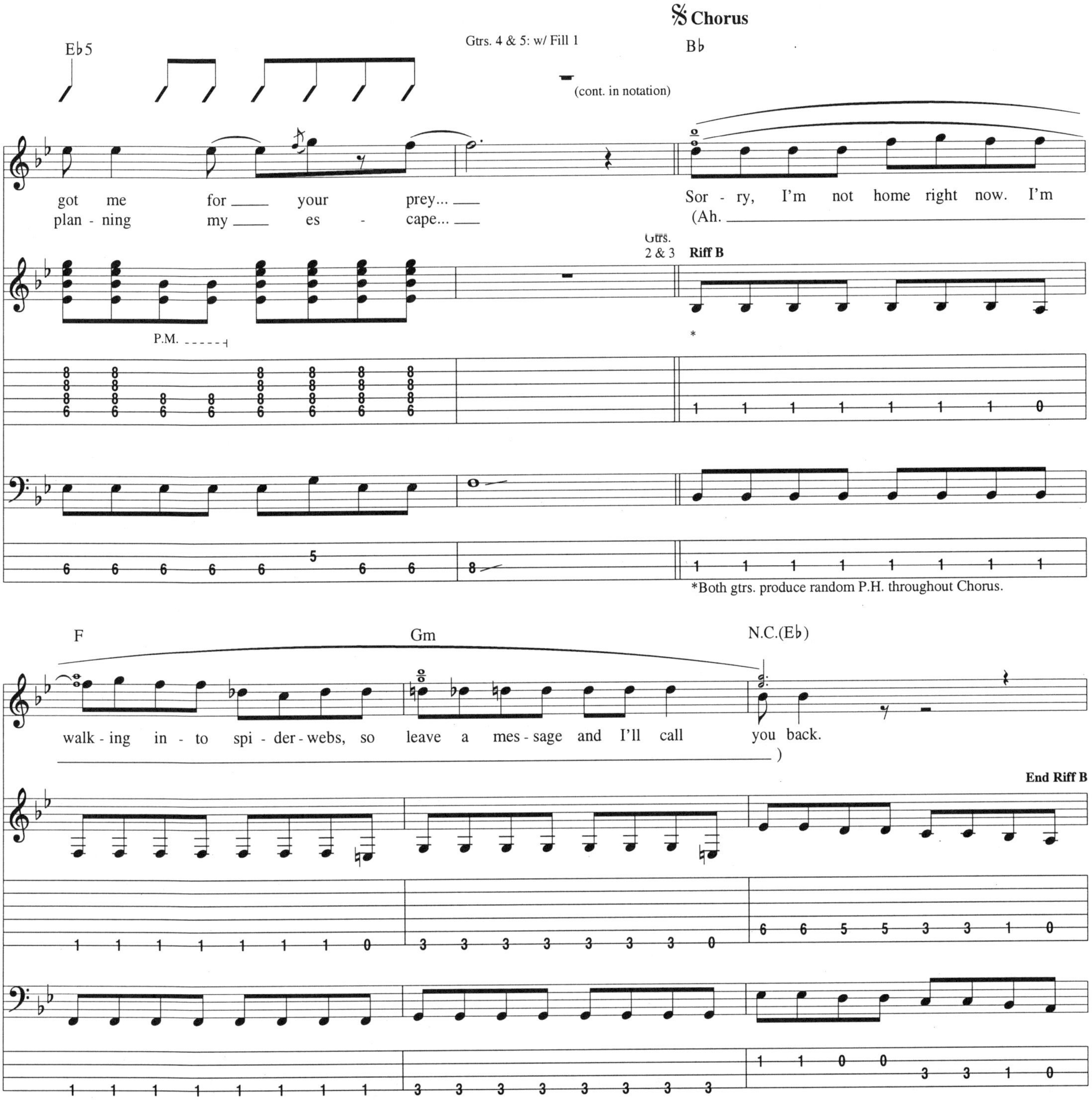

𝄋 Chorus

Eb5 | Gtrs. 4 & 5: w/ Fill 1 (cont. in notation) | Bb

got me for your prey...
plan - ning my es - cape...

Sor - ry, I'm not home right now. I'm
(Ah.

Gtrs. 2 & 3 Riff B

P.M.

*Both gtrs. produce random P.H. throughout Chorus.

F | Gm | N.C.(Eb)

walk - ing in - to spi - der - webs, so leave a mes - sage and I'll call you back.
)

End Riff B

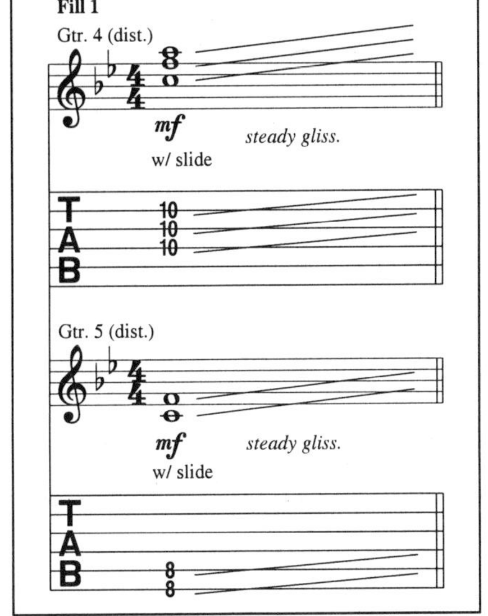

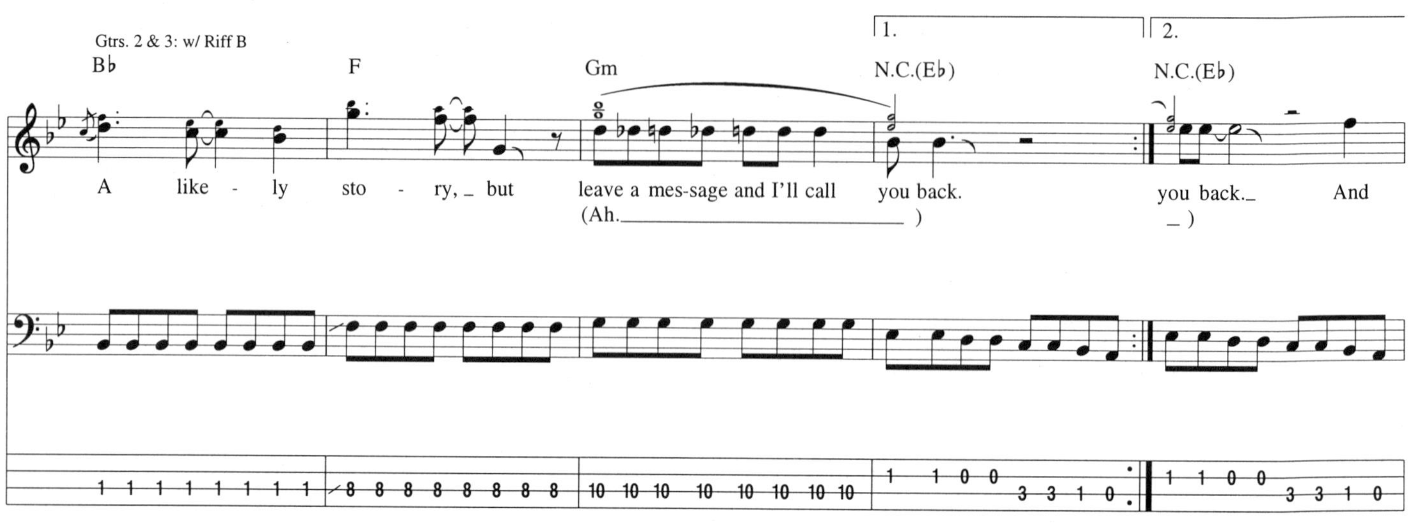
Gtrs. 2 & 3: w/ Riff B
B♭
F
Gm
1.
N.C.(E♭)
2.
N.C.(E♭)
A like - ly sto - ry, but leave a mes-sage and I'll call you back. you back. And
(Ah.)
)

B♭
F
Gm
N.C.(E♭)
it's all your fault; I screen my phone calls. No
Rhy. Fig. 1
Gtrs. 2 & 3
End Rhy. Fig. 1
Bass Fig. 3
End Bass Fig. 3

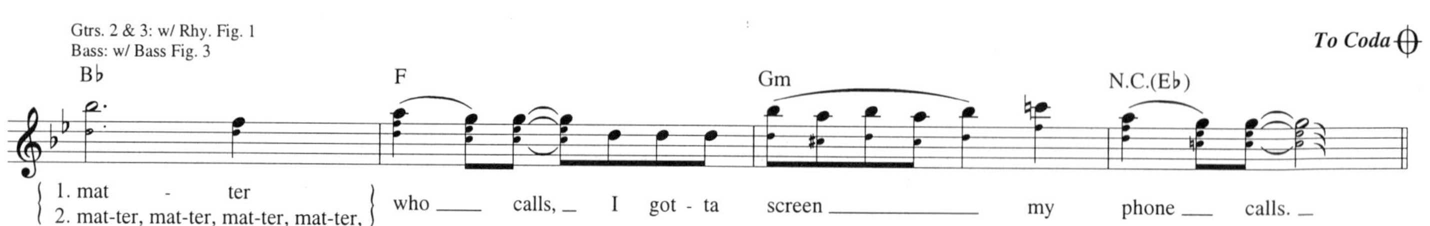
Gtrs. 2 & 3: w/ Rhy. Fig. 1
Bass: w/ Bass Fig. 3
To Coda
B♭
F
Gm
N.C.(E♭)
1. mat - ter
2. mat-ter, mat-ter, mat-ter, mat-ter,
who calls, I got - ta screen my phone calls.

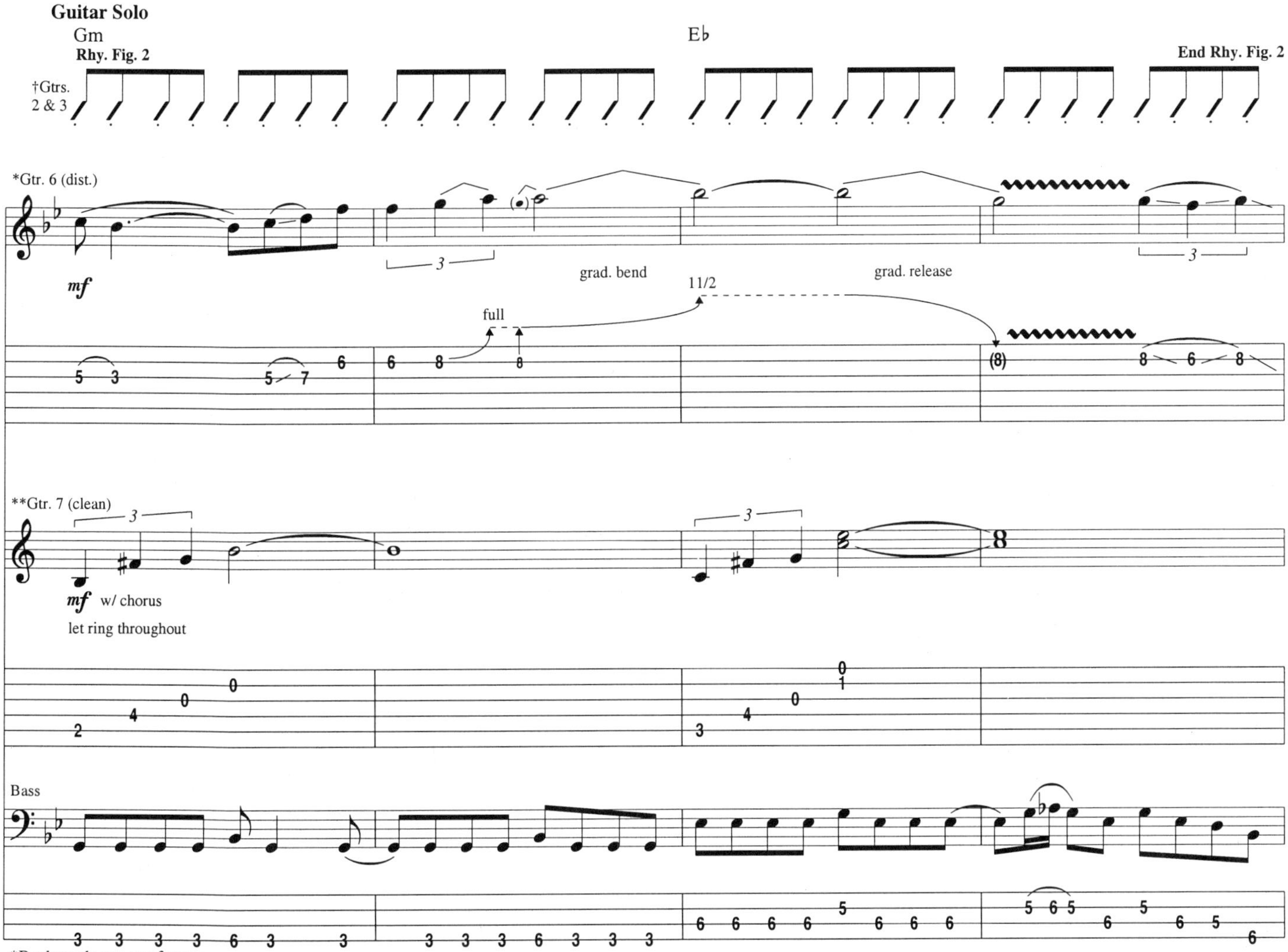

Guitar Solo
Gm
Rhy. Fig. 2
†Gtrs. 2 & 3
E♭
End Rhy. Fig. 2
*Gtr. 6 (dist.)
mf
grad. bend
grad. release
11/2
full
**Gtr. 7 (clean)
mf w/ chorus
let ring throughout
Bass

*Backwards gtr. arr. for gtr.
**Capo at 3rd fret. Capo becomes "0" in TAB.
†Rhythm is produced by switching toggle switch back & forth between on & off positions.

Gtrs. 2 & 3: w/ Rhy. Fig. 2
Gm
E♭
Gtr. 6
full
Gtr. 7

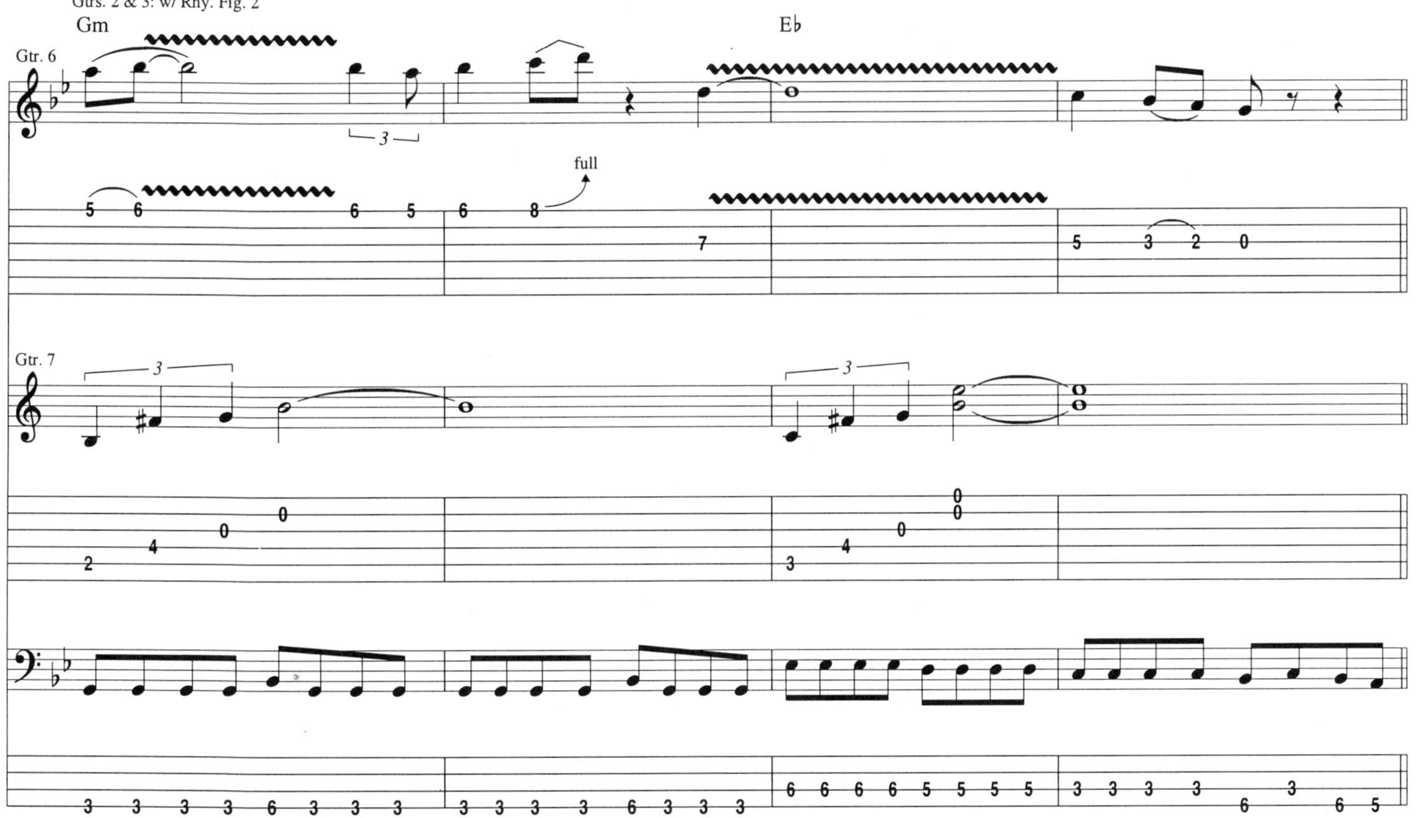

Bridge
Gtrs. 2 & 3: w/ Rhy. Fig. 2, 3 times
Gtr. 6 tacet
Gm
Eb
Now it's gone too deep. You
(Now it's gone too
Gtr. 7
Gm
Eb
wake me in my sleep. My
deep. Wake me in my
Gm
Eb
dreams be - come night - mares 'cause you're
sleep. Dreams be - come night - mares.

D.S. al Coda
(take 2nd ending)

Gtr. 7 tacet

G5 | N.C.(E♭)

ring - ing in my ears.
Ring - ing in my...)

Gtrs. 2 & 3 | Gtr. 3 | Gtrs. 2 & 3

Gtr. 2
divisi

Coda

Gtrs. 2 & 3: w/ Riff B, 5 3/4 times, simile

B♭ | F | Gm | N.C.(E♭)

Oo, a spi - der-web; leave a mes-sage and I'll call you back.

Bass **Bass Fig. 4** | **End Bass Fig. 4**

Bass: w/ Bass Fig. 4

B♭ | F | Gm | N.C.(E♭)

I'm walk-ing in - to spi - der-webs, so leave a mes-sage and I'll call you back.

w/ ad lib. Bkgd. Voc.

B♭ | F | Gm | N.C.(E♭)

It's all your fault; I screen my phone calls.

Bass Fig. 5 | **End Bass Fig. 5**

Bass: w/ Bass Fig. 5, 2 3/4 times

B♭ | F | Gm | N.C.(E♭)

No mat-ter, mat-ter, mat-ter who calls, I got-ta screen my phone calls.

B♭
F
Gm
N.C.(E♭)
It's all your fault.
It's all your fault.
No mat - ter who calls.
No mat - ter who
Outro
A Tempo
Bass: w/ Bass Fig. 1
Gtrs. 2 & 3 tacet
rit.
calls.
Oh.
I'm walk - ing in - to spi - der - webs, so
Gtrs. 2 & 3
Gtr. 2
Gtr. 3
divisi
P.H.
8va
full
pitch: D
*Gtrs. 1 & 8 (slight dist.)
mf
Bass
*composite arrangement
w/ ad lib. Lead Voc.
Bass: w/ Bass Fig. 1, simile, till fade
E♭
leave a mes - sage and I'll call you back.
I'm walk - ing in - to
Gtrs. 1 & 8
simile on repeats
Play 5 Times and Fade
spi - der - webs, ah, leave a mes - sage and I'll call you back.

Tears in Heaven

Words and Music by Eric Clapton and Will Jennings

A7/E
F♯7
F♯7sus4
F♯/A♯
Bm7
and car - ry on,
'cause I know
I don't be - long
through night and day
'cause I know
I just can't stay
To Coda
D/E
A
E/G♯
F♯m7
F♯m7/E
1.
D/F♯
E7sus4
E7
here in hea - ven.
here in hea - ven.
2.
A
D/F♯
E7sus4
E7
A
Bridge
C
G/B
Am
Time can bring ya down,
D/F♯
G
D/F♯
Em
D/F♯
G
C
G/B
Am
time can bend your knees.
Time can break your heart,

D/F♯ G D/F♯ E A/E E7
have ya beg - gin' please, beg - gin' please.
Interlude
A E/G♯ F♯m7 F♯m7/E D/F♯ A E A/E E7
A E/G♯ F♯m7 F♯m7/E D/F♯ A E A/E E7
Chorus
F♯m7 C♯/E♯ A7/E
Be - yond the door there's peace, I'm sure,

F#7
G#m
F#/A#
Bm7
D/E
and I know
there'll be
no more
tears in hea-
A
E/G#
F#m7
F#m7/E
D/F#
E7sus4
E7
ven.
T
A
Verse
A
E/G#
F#m7
F#m7/E
3. Would you know
my name
T
D/F#
A
E
A/E
E7
A
E/G#
F#m7
if I saw you in hea-ven?
Would you be the same
T
T

F♯m7/E D/F♯ A/E E A/E E7

if I saw you in hea - ven?

T

Coda

A E/G♯ F♯m7 F♯m7/E

ven. 'Cause I

T

Bm7 D/E A E/G♯ F♯m

know I don't be - long here in hea - ven.

T

F♯m/E D/F♯ E7sus4 E7 **Freely** A

rit.

let ring

rit.

T

Two Princes

Words and Music by Spin Doctors

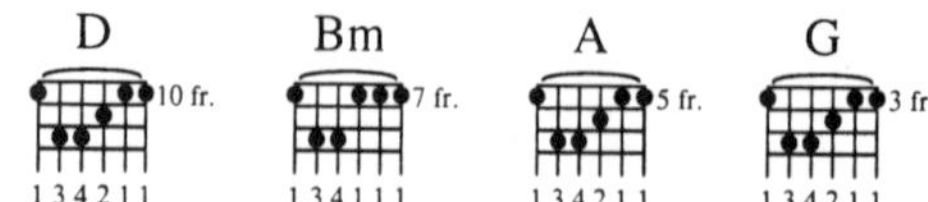

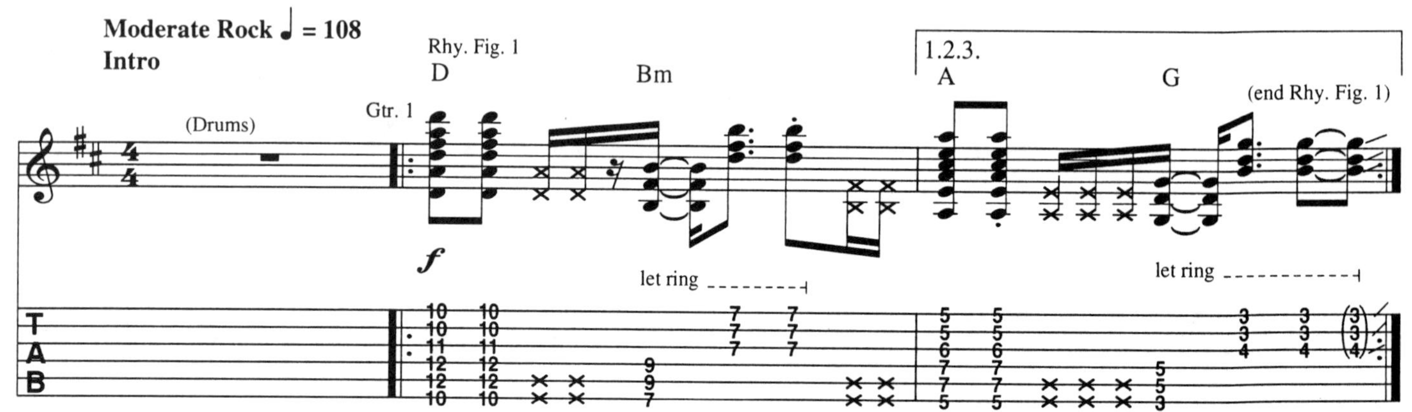

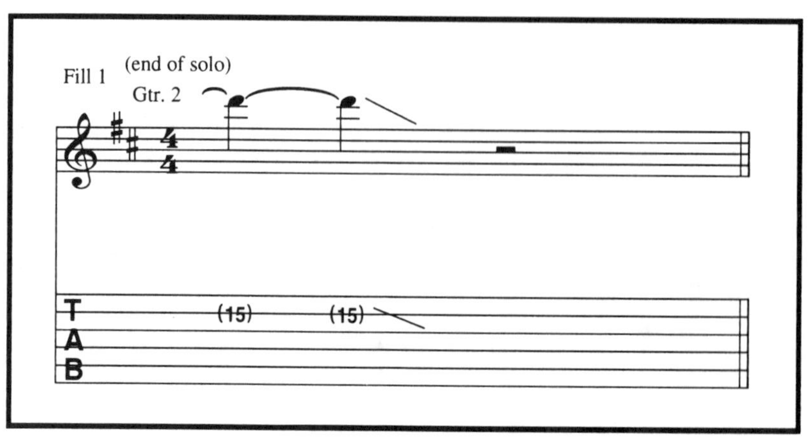

D
Bm
A
G
Princ - es, princ - es who __ a - dore ____ you. Just go a - head, __ now.
Got some big seal up - on __ his jack - et, ain't in his head, __ now. You
if you like to tell ___ me may - be, just go a - head, __ now. And
let ring
let ring
D
Bm
A
G
One has di - 'monds in ___ his pock - ets, and that's some bread, _ now.
mar - ry him, your fath - er will __ con - done ___ you, how 'bout that, _ now? You
if you wan - na buy __ me flow - ers, just go a head, _ now. And
let ring
let ring
D
Bm
A
G
3rd time to Coda I
This one, said he wants to buy __ you rock - ets, ain't in his head, _ now.
mar - ry me, your fath - er will __ dis - own ____ you, he'll eat his hat, __ now.
if you like to talk __ for hours, ____ just go a - head, __ now.
let ring
let ring

1.
D
Bm7
A
G
Yeah, yeah, yeah.
De de de
Rhy. Fig. 2
let ring
D
Bm7
A
G
dit. D-be, be be de. Be-dee-dl-y de-bu du-bu du-bu du-bu du-bu du-bu du-bu du-bu.
(end Rhy. Fig. 2)
let ring
2.
G
D
G
Mar-ry him or mar-ry me. I'm the one that loves you ba-by, can't you see? I ain't
Rhy. Fig. 3
A
2nd time to Coda II
got no fu-ture or fam-'ly tree, but I know what a prince and lov-er ought to be.
(end Rhy. Fig. 3)

D. S. al Coda I
Coda I
Guitar Solo
D
Bm
Gtr. 1
Gtr. 2
I know what a prince and lov - er ought to be. __ Said. . .
1/2
A
G
full
w/Rhy. Fig. 3 (Gtr. 1)
hold bend

A
hold bend
hold bend
full
let ring
full
full
Gtr. 1
A
D. S. (take 2nd ending) al Coda II
Said. . .
(cont. in Fill 1)
hold bend
let ring
let ring
full
full
1/2
full
1/2
full
Coda II
A
C5
A5
N.C.
D
N.C.
I know what a prince and lov - er ought to be.
Said if you want to call _ me ba -
(Gtr. tacet)
1/4
by, just go a - head, _ now. And if you like to tell _ me may - be, just go a - head _ now. And
if you wan - na buy _ me flow - ers, just go a - head, _ now. And if you like to talk _ for hours, _
w/Rhy. Fig. 2 (2 times)
D
Bm7
A
G
just go a - head, _ now. And if you want to call _ me ba - by, just go a - head, _ now. And

D Bm7 A G D Bm7
if you like to tell __ me may - be, just go a - head, _ now. And if you like to buy _ me flow -
A G D Bm7 A G
ers, just go a - head, __ now. And if you like to talk __ for hours, ____ just go a - head, __now.
D Bm A G
w/Rhy. Fig. 1 (4 times)
If you want to call me ___ ba - by, just go a - head, __ now.
D Bm A G
And if you'd like to tell ___ me ____ may - be, just go a - head, ___ now.
D Bm A G D Bm
If you want to buy me flow - ers, just go a - head, __ now. And if you like to talk for hours, _
A G D Bm7 A G
w/Rhy. Fig. 2 (2 times)
___ just go a - head, _ now. Oh, ______ ba - by. Oh, _
(Just go a - head, _ now.)
D Bm7 A G D Bm7
_____ oh, ______ just, just go a - head, ___ now. Oh, ______ your __ maj -
(Just go a - head, ___now.)
A G D Bm7
es - ty, ______ come on __ for - get ___ the king ___ and
(Just go a - head, __ now.)
A G D Bm7 A G
w/Rhy. Fig. 1
(cont. Lead voc. ad lib)
Repeat and fade
mar - ry me. ______
(Just go a - head, __ now.)
(Just go a - head, __ now.)

What I Got

Words and Music by Brad Nowell, Eric Wilson and Floyd Gaugh

D5 G5 D5 G5 D5 G5
Got to find a rea - son why my mon-ey's all gone. I got a Dal - ma - tion, and
D5 G5 D5 G5 D5 G5
I can still get high. I can play the gui - tar like a moth - er - fuck - in' ri - ot.
Gtr. 2 (acous.)
Fill 1
End Fill 1
Gtr. 1
End Riff A
P.S.
* Pick slide unintentionally sounds open strings.
Interlude
w/ Voc. ad lib.
Gtr. 1: w/ Riff A, 1st 4 meas. only, simile
D5 G5 D5 G5 D5 G5 D5 G5
2. Well, life
Gtr. 2
grad. bend
1/4
let ring
3/4
** Tap gtr. body

Verse
Gtr. 1: w/ Riff A, simile
Gtr. 2 tacet
D5
G5
D5
G5
is (too short) so love the one you got 'cause you might get run o - ver or you might get shot.
3. Why, I don't cry when my dog runs a - way. I don't get an - gry at the bills I have to pay.

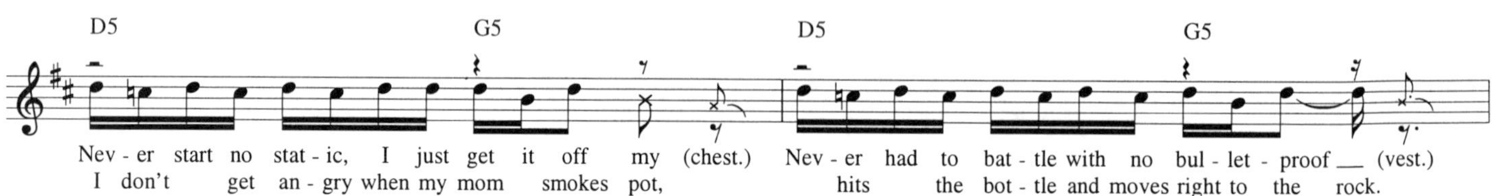
D5
G5
D5
G5
Nev - er start no stat - ic, I just get it off my (chest.) Nev - er had to bat - tle with no bul - let - proof (vest.)
I don't get an - gry when my mom smokes pot, hits the bot - tle and moves right to the rock.

D5
G5
D5
G5
Take a small ex - am - ple, take a ti - ti - ti-tip from me. Take all of your mon - ey, give it all... Love
(to char - i - ty - ty - ty - ty.)
Fuck-in' and fight-in', it's all the same. Liv - in' with Lou - ie Dog's the on - ly way to stay sane.

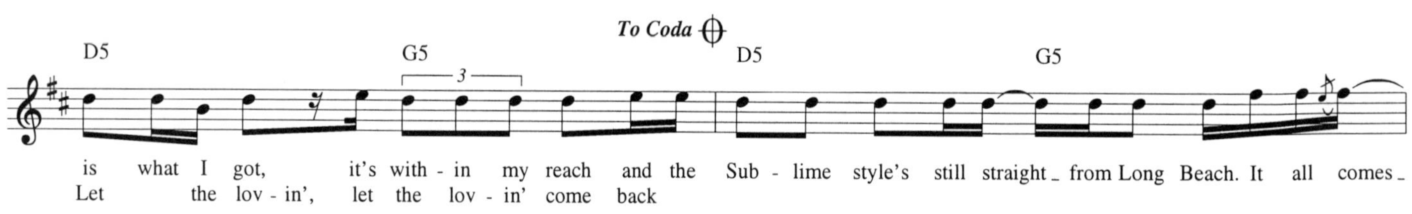
To Coda
D5
G5
3
D5
G5
is what I got, it's with - in my reach and the Sub - lime style's still straight from Long Beach. It all comes
Let the lov - in', let the lov - in' come back

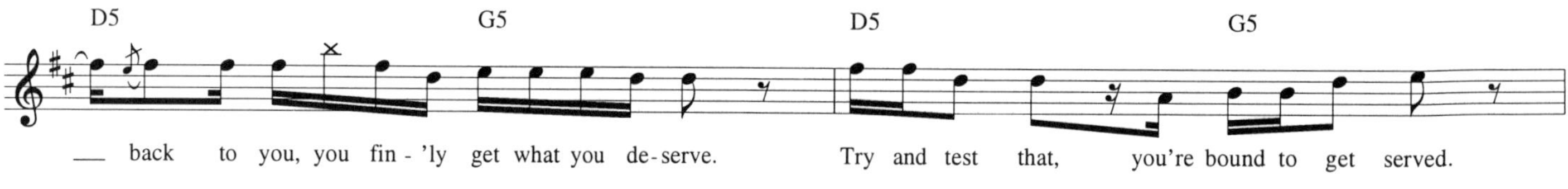
D5
G5
D5
G5
back to you, you fin - 'ly get what you de - serve. Try and test that, you're bound to get served.

D5
G5
3
Gtr. 2: w/ Fill 1
D5
G5
Love's what I got, don't start a ri - ot. You feel it when the dance gets hot.

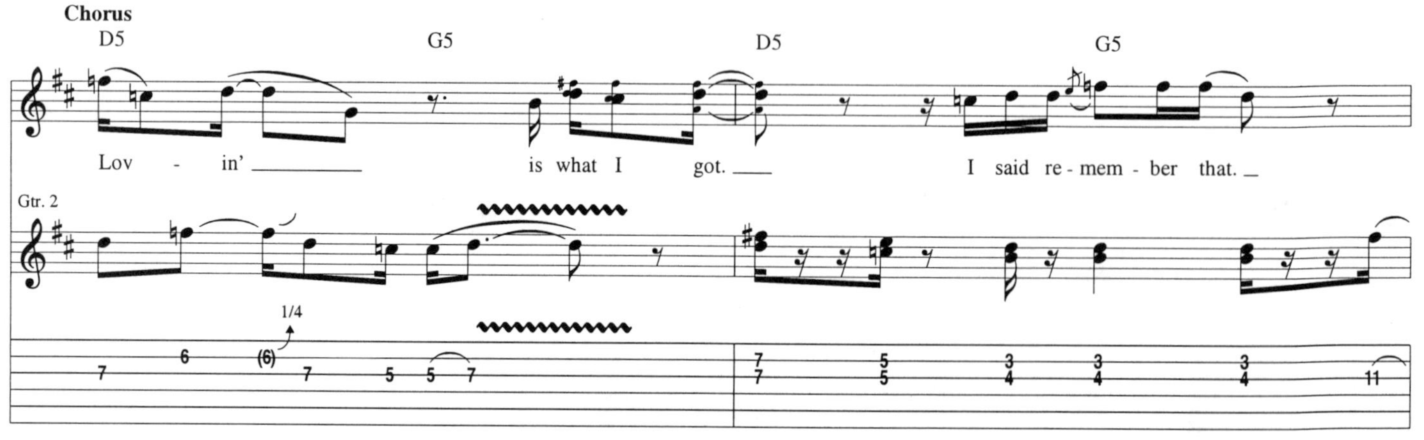
Chorus
D5
G5
D5
G5
Lov - in' is what I got. I said re - mem - ber that.
Gtr. 2
1/4

D5
G5
D5
G5
Lov - in' is what I got, and re-mem - ber that.
1/2
1/2
D5
G5
D5
G7
Lov - in' is what I got. I said re-mem - ber that.
Gtr. 2
mf
let ring
let ring
let ring
Gtr. 1
D
G5
D
G7
D.S. al Coda
Lov - in' is what I got, I got, I got, I got.
let ring
1/4
let ring

Coda
D5
Interlude
D5 C5 G5 D5 C5 G5
to me.
Riff B
D5 C5 G5 D5 C5 G5 D5
'Cause
End Riff B
Chorus
D5 C5 G5 D5 C5 G5
lov - in' is what I got. I said re-mem - ber that. Lov -
P.S.
string noise
Gtr. 1: w/ Riff B, last 2 meas. only, simile
D5 C5 G5 D5 C5 G5
Gtr. 1: w/ Riff B, simile
D5 C5 G5
- in' is what I got, and re-mem- ber that. Lov - in' is what I got.
D5 C5 G5 D5 C5 G5 D5 C5 G5
I said re-mem-ber that. Lov - in' is what I got, I got, I got, I got.
Outro
Slower ♩ = 88
D5 G5 D5 G7 D N.C. D5
Gtr. 1

What Would You Say

Words and Music by David J. Matthews

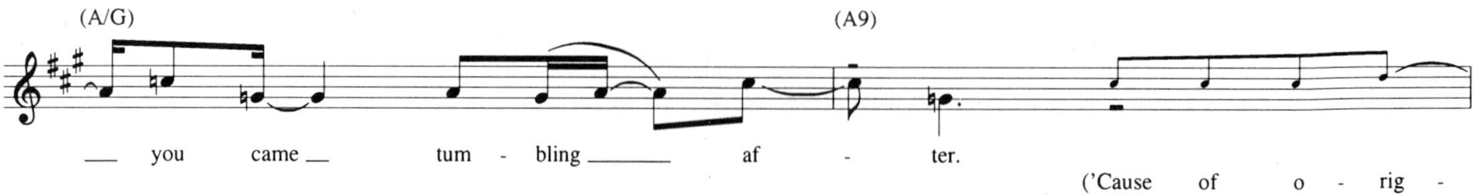

(A/G)
(A9)
you came tumbling after.
('Cause of orig-

Pre-Chorus
Gtrs. 1 & 2: w/ Rhy. Fill 1, 2nd time
Gsus2
F
G
Gtr. 1
-inal sin.)
1. Rip away the tears,
2., 4. I don't understand, at best and
Gtr. 2

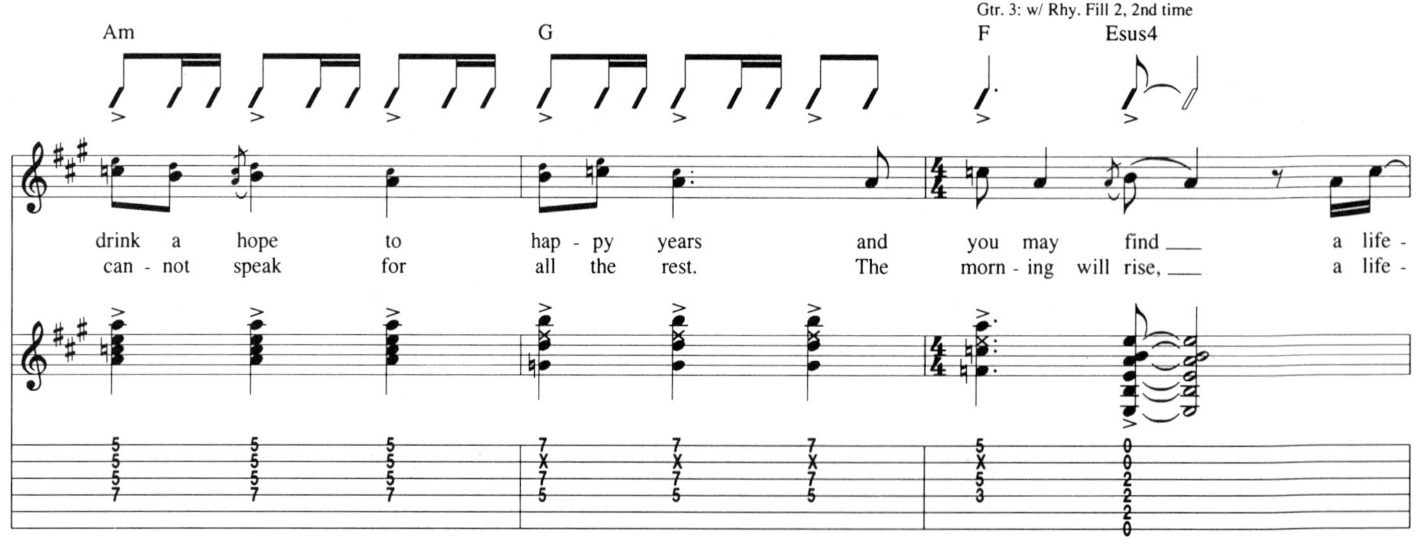

Am
G
Gtr. 3: w/ Rhy. Fill 2, 2nd time
F
Esus4
drink a hope to happy years and you may find a life-
cannot speak for all the rest. The morning will rise, a life-

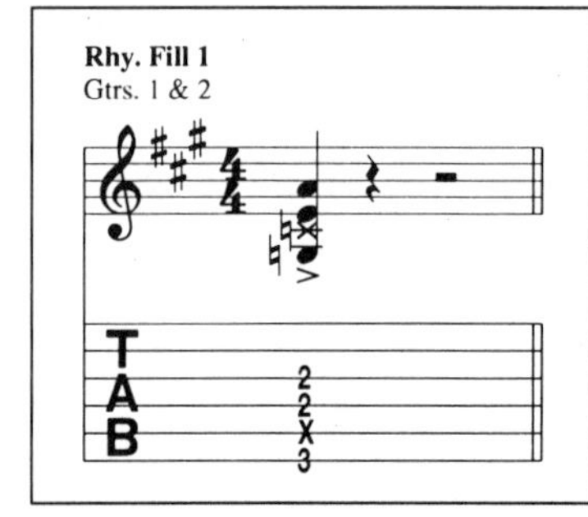

Rhy. Fill 1
Gtrs. 1 & 2

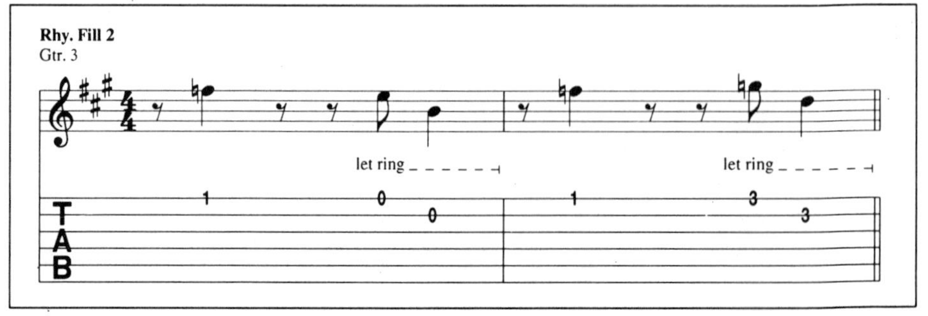

Rhy. Fill 2
Gtr. 3
let ring
let ring

Gtr. 2 tacet
F
G
N.C.(A9)
To Coda
Asus2/G
(cont. in notation)
time's passed you by.
- time's passed _ me by.
(What _ would you say? _
Gtr. 3 (acous.)
mf
let ring
Gtrs. 1 & 2
P.M.
Chorus
Gtrs. 1 & 2: w/ Rhy. Figs. 1 & 1A, 2nd time
A9
Gadd2
Don't drop the big one.
If you a mon - key on a
Rhy. Fig. 2
P.M.
Gtr. 2
Gtr. 1
divisi
End Rhy. Fig. 2
* Gtr. 1 tabbed to right of slash.

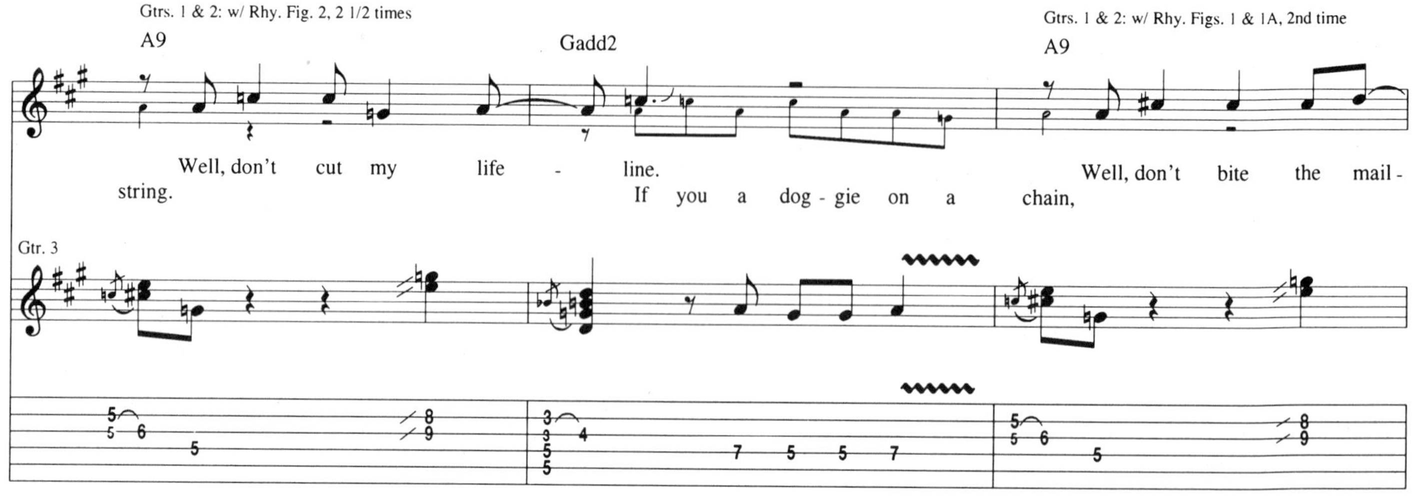
Gtrs. 1 & 2: w/ Rhy. Fig. 2, 2 1/2 times
A9
Gadd2
Gtrs. 1 & 2: w/ Rhy. Figs. 1 & 1A, 2nd time
A9
Well, don't cut my life - line.
string.
Well, don't bite the mail -
If you a dog - gie on a chain,
Gtr. 3

1.
Gadd2
A9
Gtr. 3 tacet
A/G
Gtr. 2
- man.
What would you say?)
Gtr. 1

2.
A9
A/G
Gtr. 3 tacet
Verse
A9
3. Ev - 'ry dog has its day, ev-'ry
)
Gtr. 3
Gtr. 1
P.M.
Gtrs. 1 & 2
Gtr. 2
P.M.

A/G
A9
G6
day has its way of be-ing for - got - ten.
*Mom, its my birth - day. Would you say,
P.M.
* lead voc. is doubled, next 5 meas.
A9
G6/9
** A9
G6/9
hey?
(Now, what would you say?)
What would you say?
Gtrs. 1 & 2
** w/ crowd noises
Interlude
* A7sus4
A7
A5
A(♭9)
B7
N.C.
Gtr. 1
Gtr. 2
* Chord symbols reflect combined tonality.

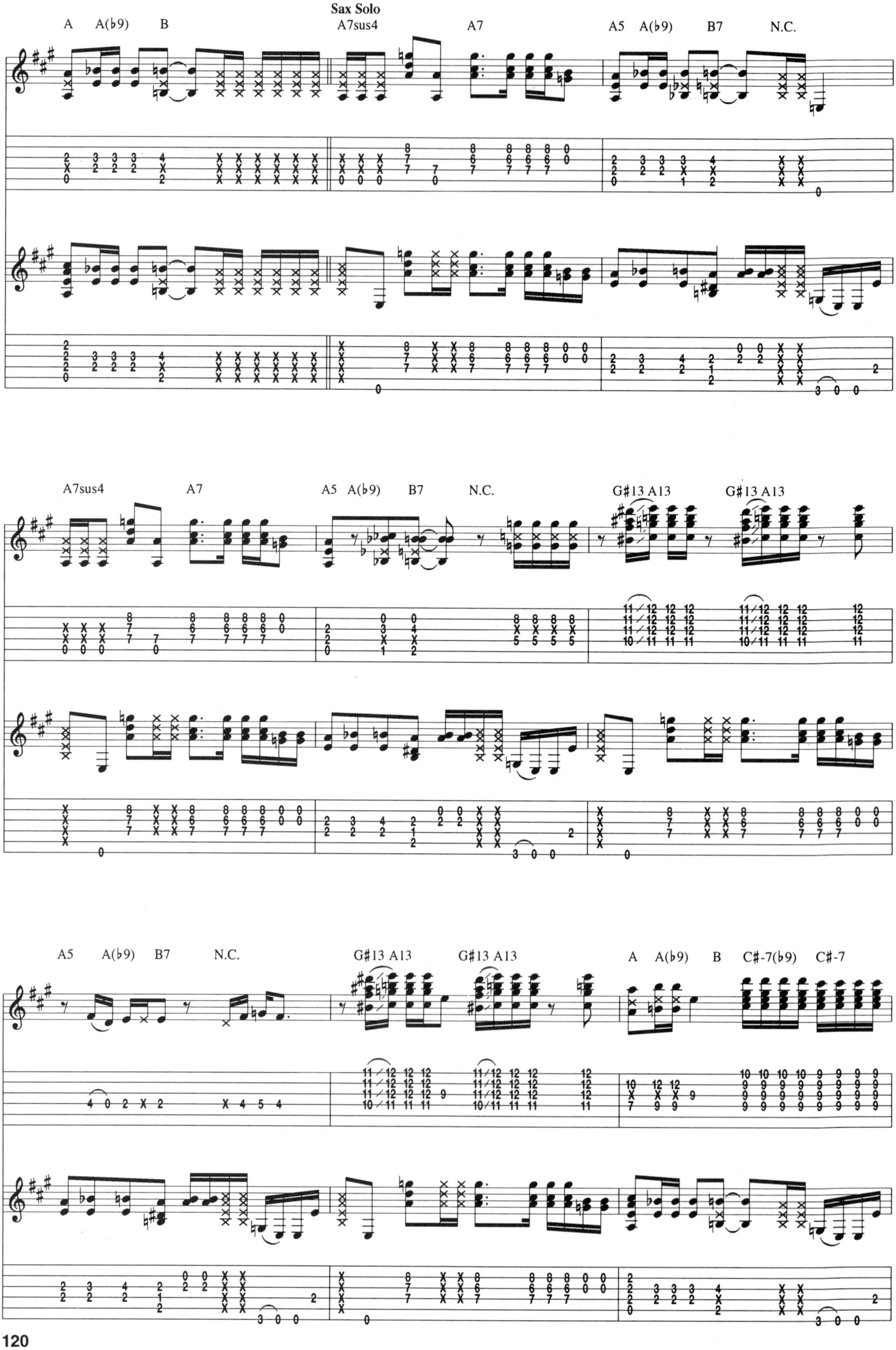

Sax Solo
A A(♭9) B A7sus4 A7 A5 A(♭9) B7 N.C.
A7sus4 A7 A5 A(♭9) B7 N.C. G#13 A13 G#13 A13
A5 A(♭9) B7 N.C. G#13 A13 G#13 A13 A A(♭9) B C#-7(♭9) C#-7

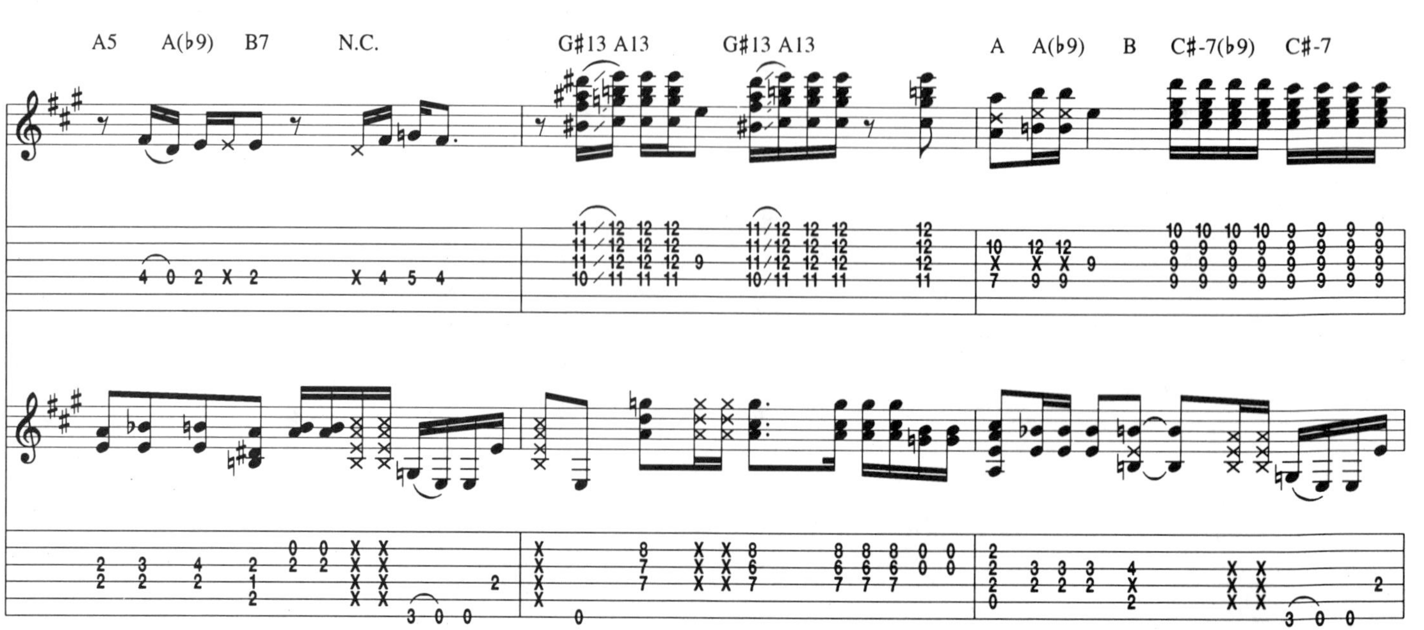

Additional Lyrics

2., 4. I was there when the bear ate his head, thought it was a candy.
(Everyone goes in the end.)
Knock, knock on the door. Who's it for? There's nobody in here.
(Look in the mirror, my friend.)

from *What's the Story Morning Glory*

Wonderwall

Words and Music by Noel Gallagher

Cadd9
21 34
Em7
12 34
G
21 34
Em7/B
12 34
Em11
34

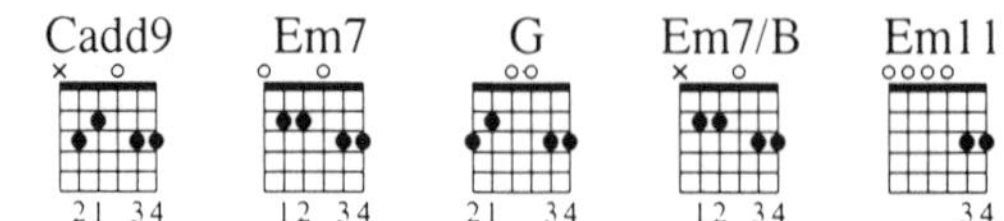

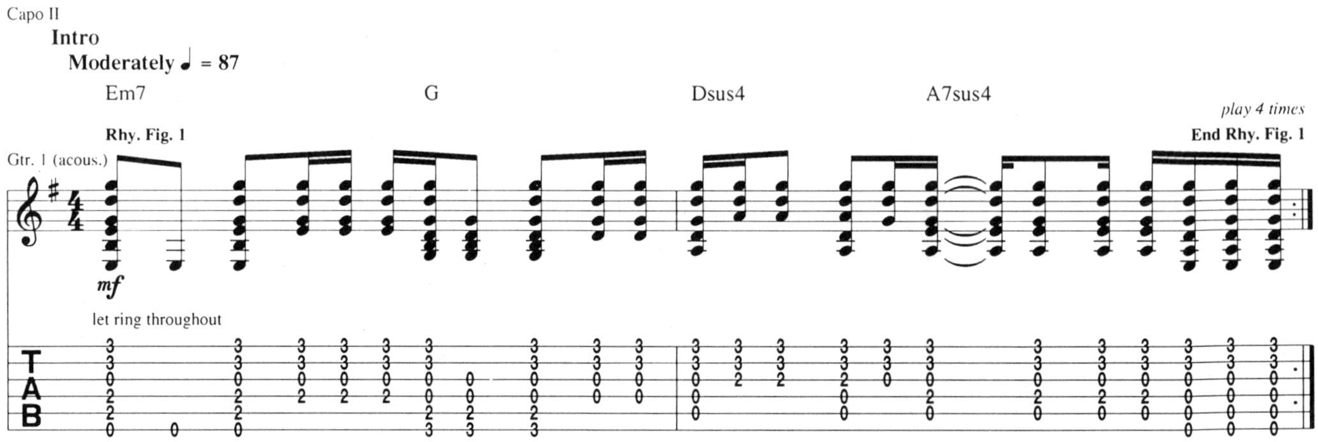

Capo II
Intro
Moderately ♩ = 87
Em7
G
Dsus4
A7sus4
play 4 times
Rhy. Fig. 1
End Rhy. Fig. 1
Gtr. 1 (acous.)
mf
let ring throughout

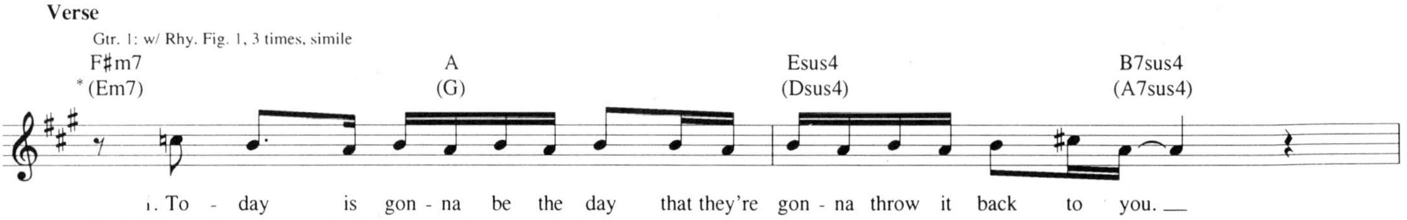

Verse
Gtr. 1: w/ Rhy. Fig. 1, 3 times, simile
F♯m7
*(Em7)
A
(G)
Esus4
(Dsus4)
B7sus4
(A7sus4)
1. To - day is gon - na be the day that they're gon - na throw it back to you.

* Symbols in parentheses represent chord names respective to capoed guitars.
Symbols above reflect actual sounding chords.

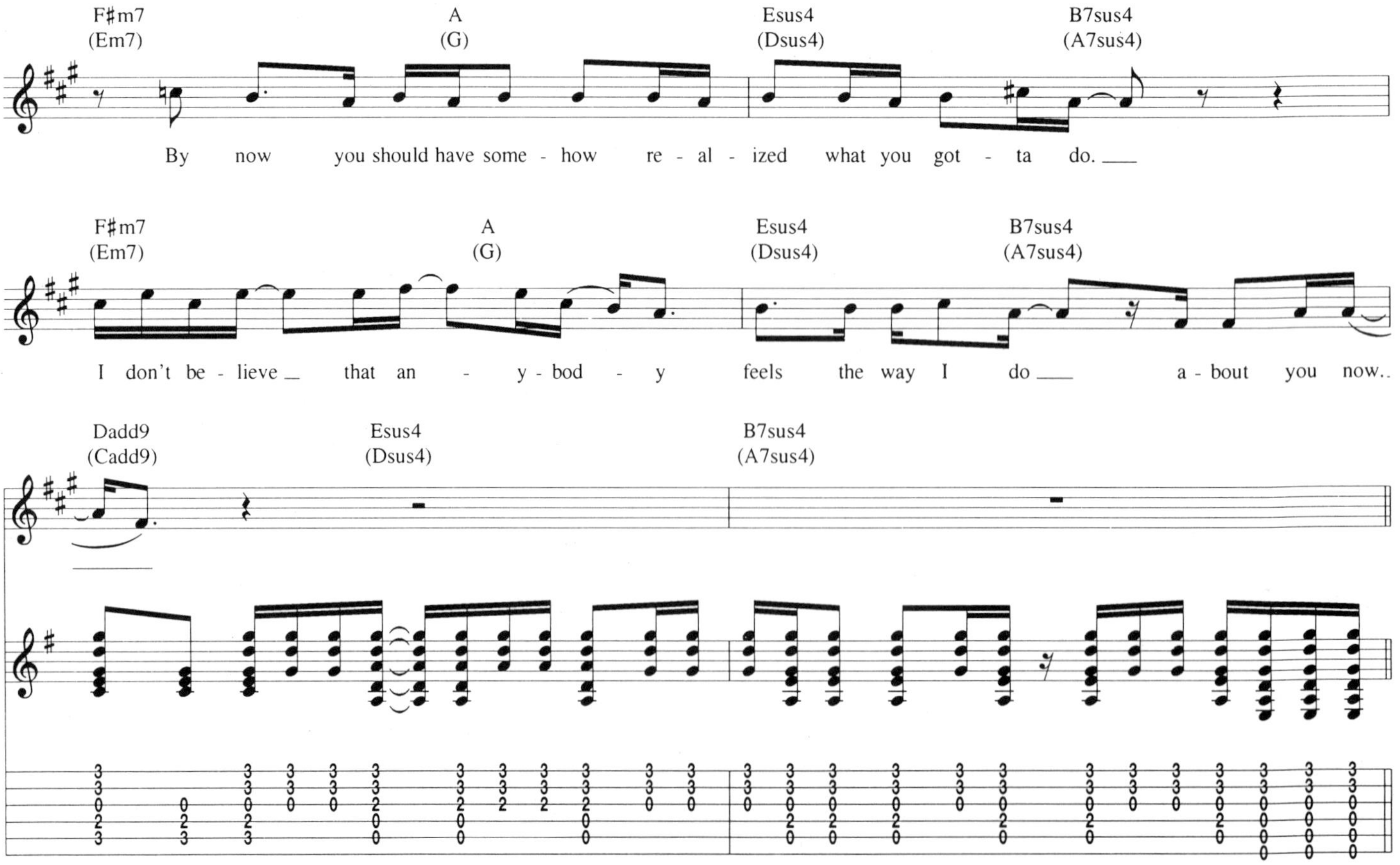

F♯m7
(Em7)
A
(G)
Esus4
(Dsus4)
B7sus4
(A7sus4)
By now you should have some - how re - al - ized what you got - ta do.
F♯m7
(Em7)
A
(G)
Esus4
(Dsus4)
B7sus4
(A7sus4)
I don't be - lieve that an - y - bod - y feels the way I do a - bout you now..
Dadd9
(Cadd9)
Esus4
(Dsus4)
B7sus4
(A7sus4)

Verse
Gtr. 1: w/ Rhy. Fig. 1, 4 times, simile
F#m7 (Em7) A (G) Esus4 (Dsus4) B7sus4 (A7sus4)
2. Back - beat, the word is on the street that the fire ___ in your heart is out. ___
3. To - day was gon - na be the day, but they'll nev - er throw it back to you. ___
I'm sure you've heard it all be - fore, but you nev - er real - ly had a doubt. _
By now you should have some - how re - al - ized what you're not to do. ___
I don't be - lieve _ that an - y - bod - y feels the way I do ___ a - bout you now. _
And all ___
And all ___
Pre-Chorus
*D (C) E (D) F#m7 (Em7)
___ the roads _ we have _ to walk _ are wind - ing, and all _
___ the roads _ that lead _ you there _ were wind - ing, and all _
Gtrs. 1 & 2 (clean)
mf
let ring throughout
* Chord symbols reflect overall tonality.
D (C) E (D) F#m7 (Em7)
___ the lights _ that lead _ us there _ are blind - ing.
___ the lights _ that light _ the way _ are blind - ing.

D
(C)
E
(D)
A
(G)
E/G♯
(D/F♯)
F♯m7
(Em7)
A
(G)
There are man - y things that I would like to say to you, but I don't know how.

B7sus4
(A7sus4)
Be-cause
I said
(cont. in slash)

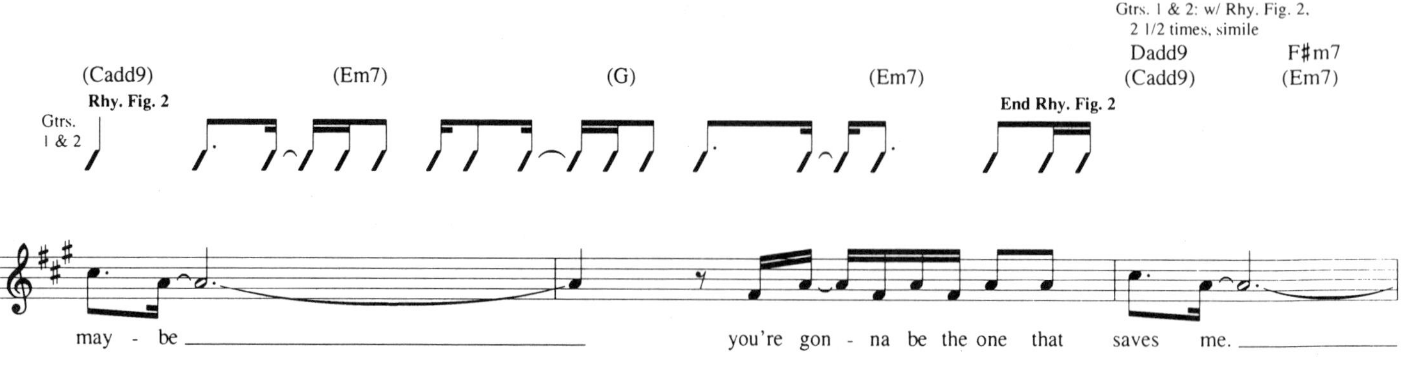
Gtrs. 1 & 2: w/ Rhy. Fig. 2, 2 1/2 times, simile
(Cadd9)
(Em7)
(G)
(Em7)
Dadd9
(Cadd9)
F♯m7
(Em7)
Rhy. Fig. 2
End Rhy. Fig. 2
Gtrs. 1 & 2
may - be you're gon - na be the one that saves me.

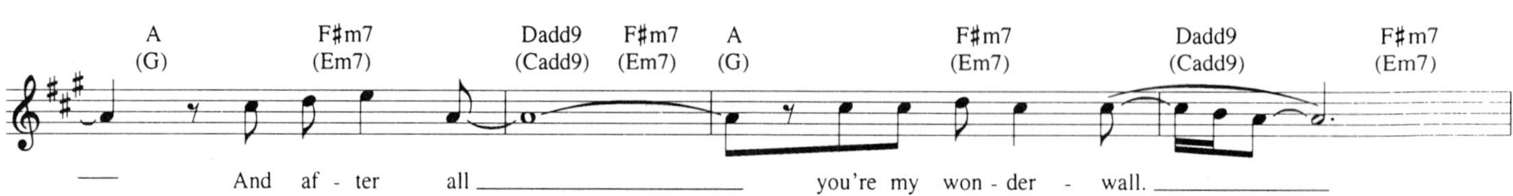
A
(G)
F♯m7
(Em7)
Dadd9
(Cadd9)
F♯m7
(Em7)
A
(G)
F♯m7
(Em7)
Dadd9
(Cadd9)
F♯m7
(Em7)
And af - ter all you're my won - der - wall.

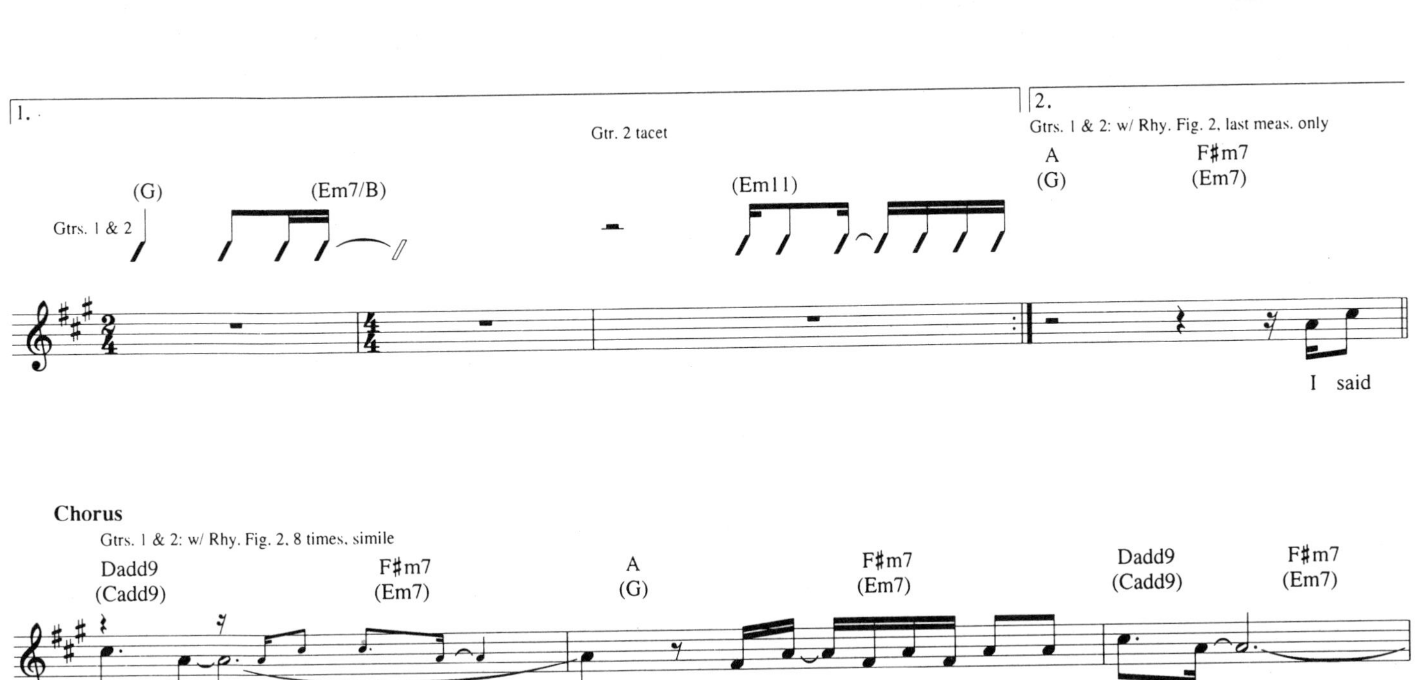
1.
Gtr. 2 tacet
2.
Gtrs. 1 & 2: w/ Rhy. Fig. 2, last meas. only
(G)
(Em7/B)
(Em11)
A
(G)
F#m7
(Em7)
Gtrs. 1 & 2
I said

Chorus

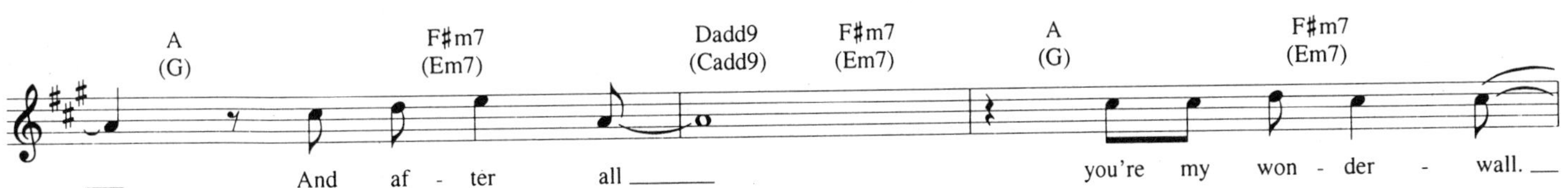
Gtrs. 1 & 2: w/ Rhy. Fig. 2, 8 times, simile
Dadd9
(Cadd9)
F#m7
(Em7)
A
(G)
may - be
(I said may - be.)
you're gon - na be the one that saves me.

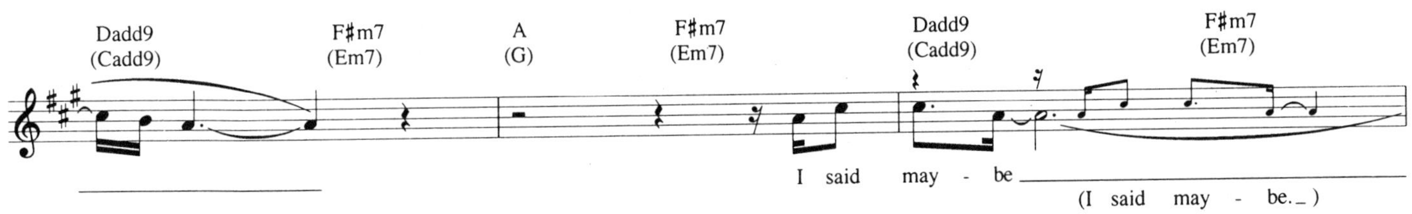
A
(G)
F#m7
(Em7)
Dadd9
(Cadd9)
And af - ter all
you're my won - der - wall.

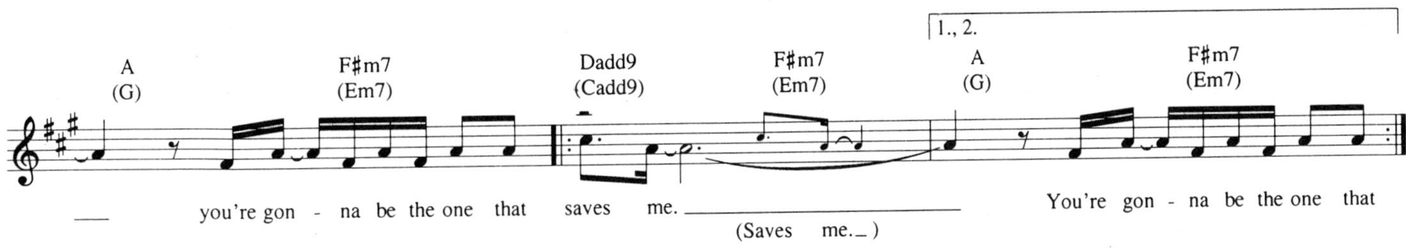
Dadd9
(Cadd9)
F#m7
(Em7)
A
(G)
I said may - be
(I said may - be.)
1., 2.
you're gon - na be the one that saves me.
(Saves me.)
You're gon - na be the one that

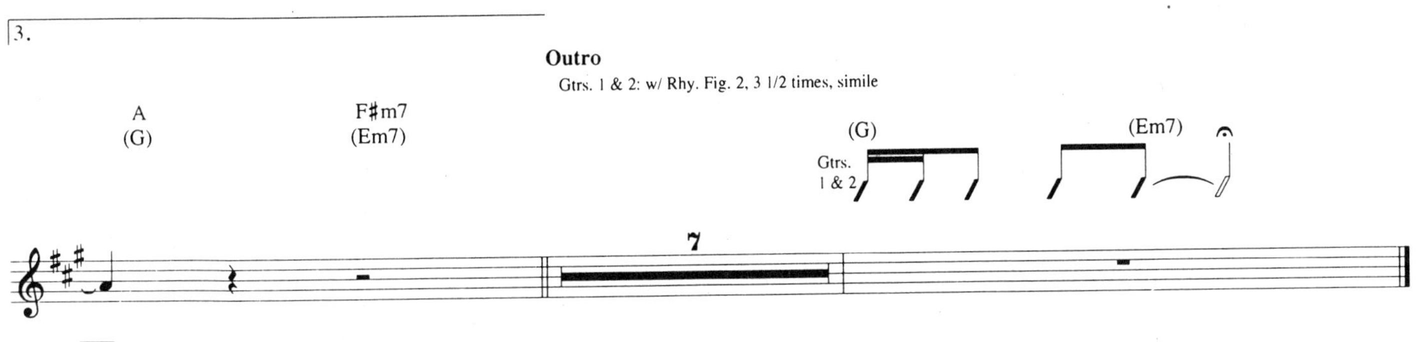
3.
Outro
Gtrs. 1 & 2: w/ Rhy. Fig. 2, 3 1/2 times, simile
A
(G)
F#m7
(Em7)
(G)
(Em7)
Gtrs. 1 & 2
7

You Oughta Know

Lyrics by Alanis Morissette
Music by Alanis Morissette and Glen Ballard

MCA Music Publishing

Pre-Chorus
F#m7
Rhy. Fig. 1
Gtr. 3 (fuzz)
mf
1., 2. love that you gave, that we made was-n't a - ble to make it e-nough for you to be o - pen wide, no.
3. joke that you laid in the bed that was me and I'm not gon-na fade as soon as you close your eyes, and you know it.
And ev -
And ev -
Gtr. 1
Gtr. 2 (clean)
mp
let ring throughout
B
End Rhy. Fig. 1

Gtr. 3: w/ Rhy. Fig. 1
F♯m7
- 'ry time _ you speak _ her name _ does she know _ how you told _ me you'd hold me un - til
- 'ry time _ I scratch _ my nails _ down some - one else-'s back, I hope you
B
you died, 'til you died? But your still a - live. And I'm here
feel it. Well, can you feel it? Well, I'm here
(cont. in slash)
Chorus
F♯
Rhy. Fig. 2
Gtr. 1
E
A
B
End Rhy. Fig. 2
to re - mind you of the mess you left _ when you went a-way. It's not
Gtr. 3
Rhy. Fig. 2B
End Rhy. Fig. 2B
Gtr. 2
Rhy. Fig. 2A
End Rhy. Fig. 2A
mf

To Coda 1 ⊕

To Coda 2 ⊕

Gtrs. 1, 2 & 3: w/ Rhy. Figs. 2, 2A & 2B

F♯ E A B

fair __ to de - ny __ me of the cross __ I bear _ that you gave to me. You, _ you, _ you

Verse

Gtr. 2 tacet

B^II F♯m7^II B/F♯

Gtr. 1 Gtr. 3

(cont. in notation)

mp

ought-a know. _ 2. You seem ve - ry well, things look peace -

Gtr. 3 (Gtr. 3 cont. in slash) Gtr. 1

Gtr. 2 *divisi*

11 12/ 4 11/ 4 4 2 | 2 4 2 4 | 2 4 | 4 4 4 5

F♯m7^II B/F♯

- ful. I'm not quite _ as well, I thought __ you __ should know. _

(5) 2 4 4 2 | 2 2 2 5 4 2 5 | 2 2 4 | 4 4 4 5

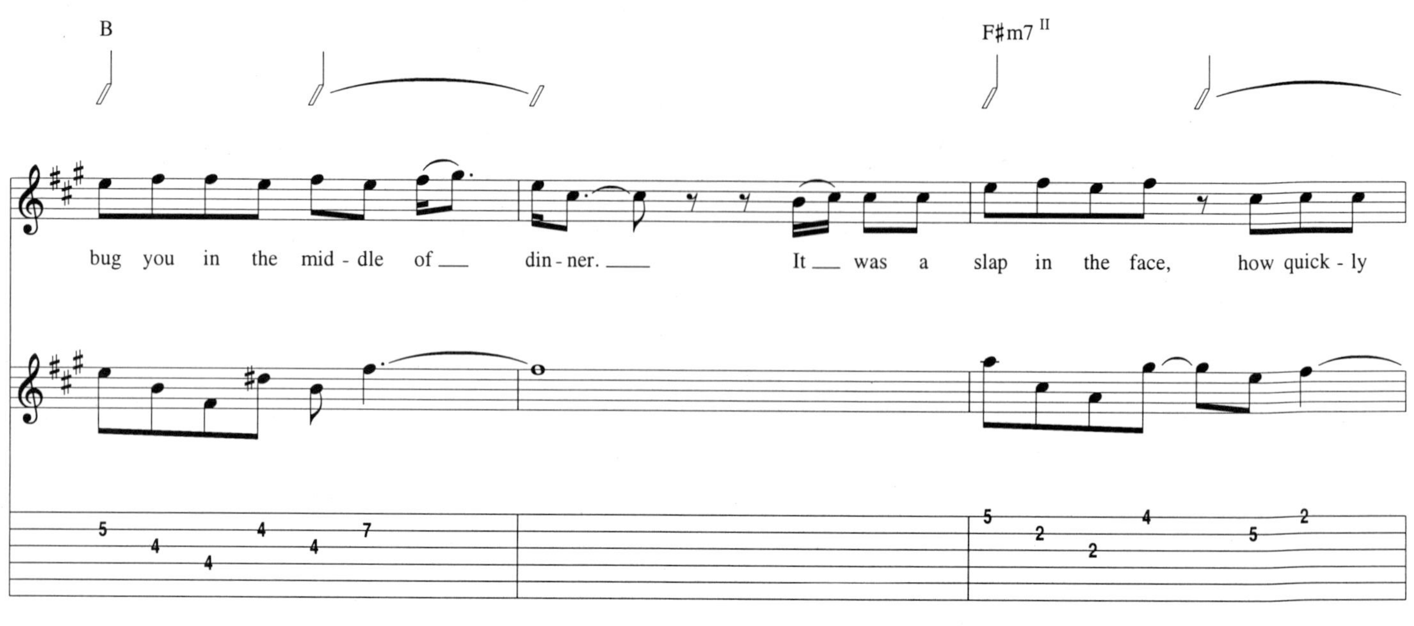
B
F♯m7 II
bug you in the mid - dle of ___ din - ner. ___ It ___ was a slap in the face, how quick - ly

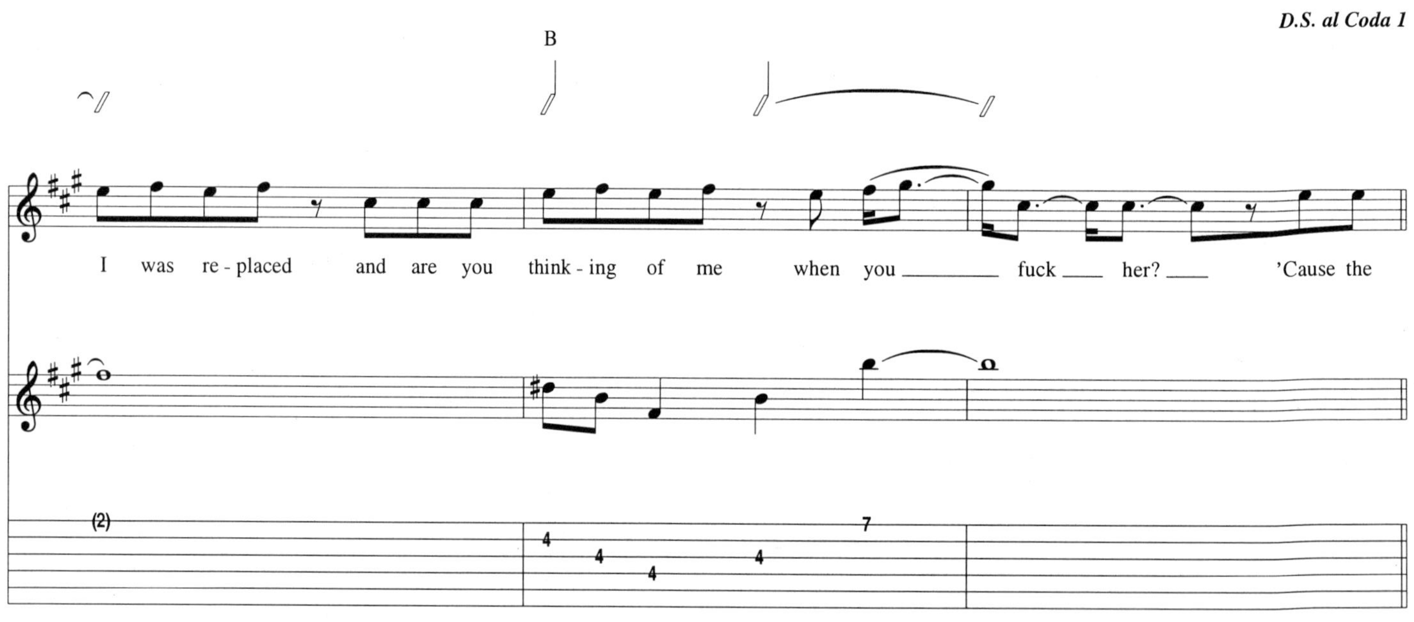
D.S. al Coda 1
B
I was re - placed and are you think - ing of me when you ________ fuck ___ her? ___ 'Cause the

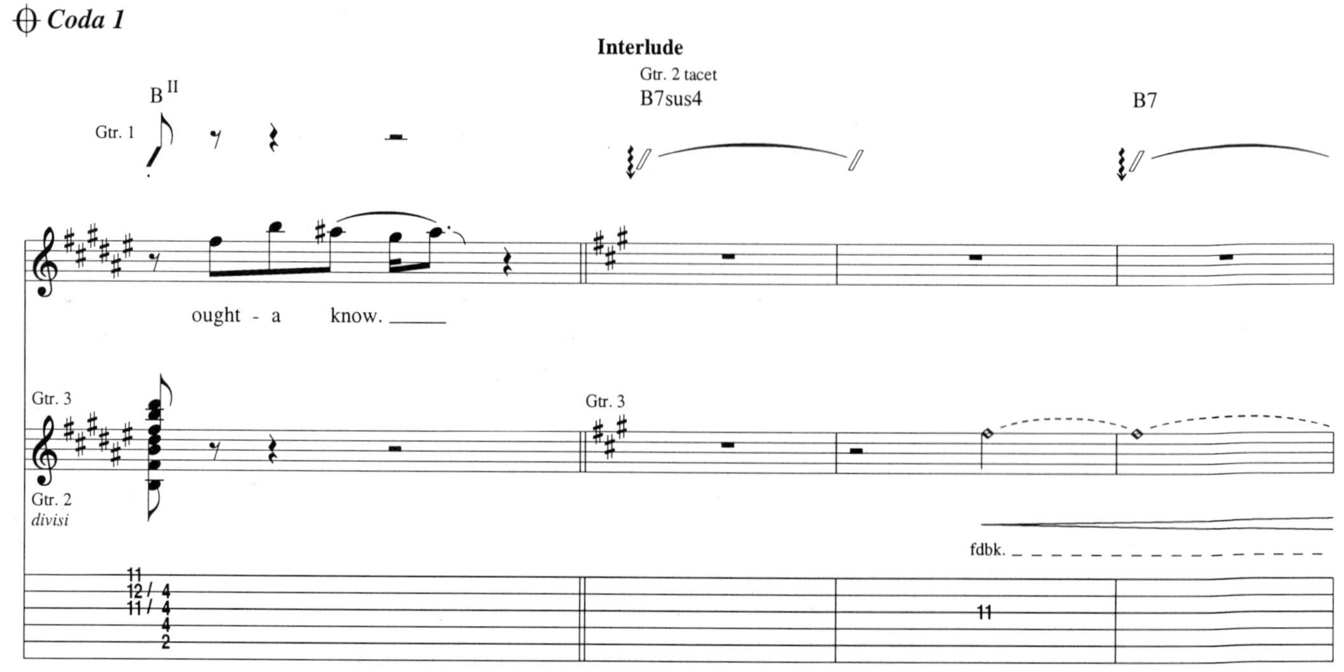
Coda 1
Interlude
Gtr. 2 tacet
B II
Gtr. 1
B7sus4
B7
ought - a know. _____
Gtr. 3
Gtr. 2
divisi
fdbk.

B7sus4
Ah.
w/ bar
w/ bar
fdbk.
(11)
-1
pitch: E
-1/2
D♯
-1
D
B7
F♯m/B
Ah.
Ah.
fdbk.
fdbk.
(0)
-3/4
-1
-1/2
-1/2
pitch: E
D♯
pitch: D♯
C♯
Gtr. 3 tacet
B type2
B7
Ah.
Ah.
Ah.
D.S. al Coda 2
F♯m/B
Ah.
Ah.
Ah.
'Cause the

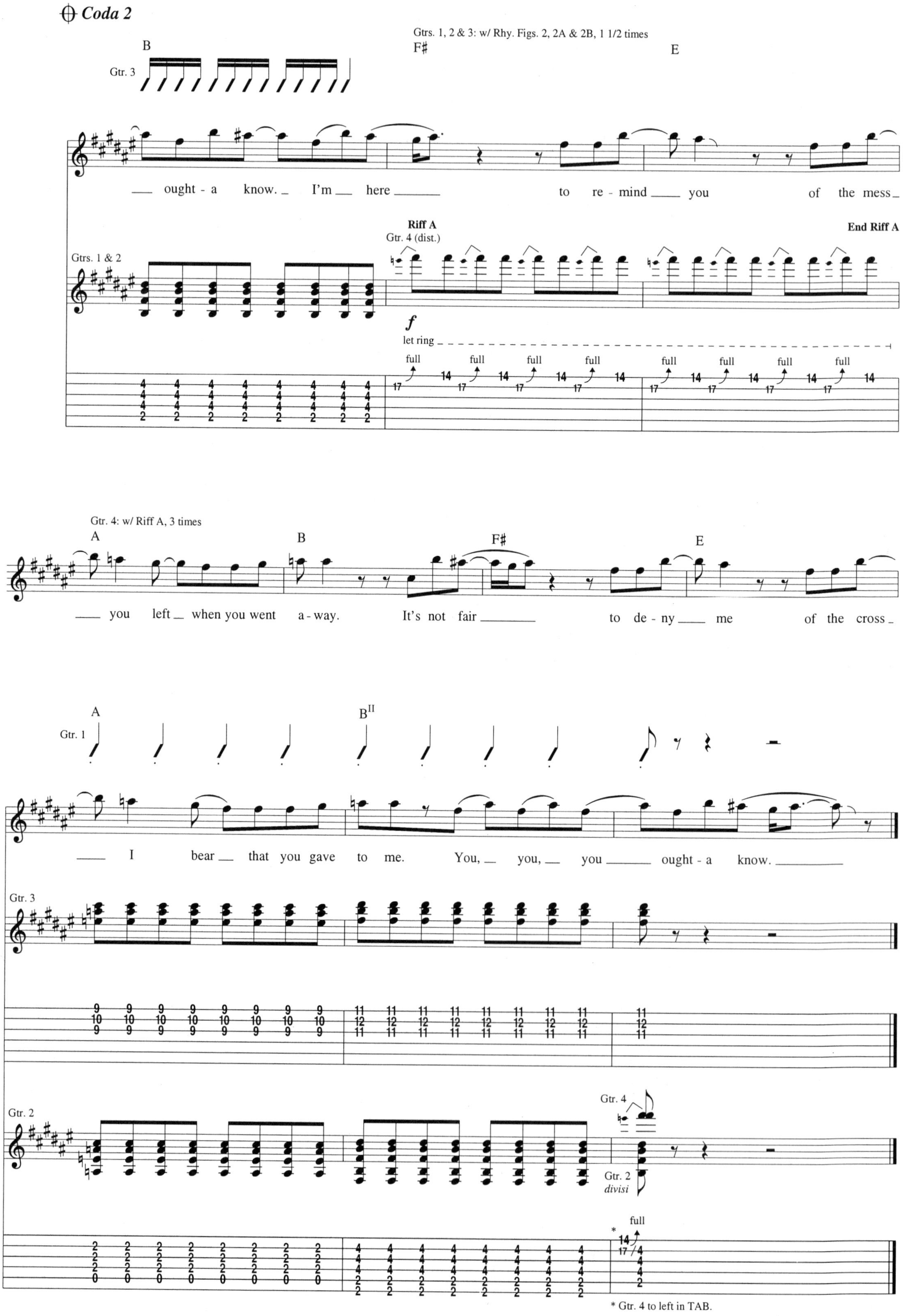

Coda 2

A

B[II]

Gtr. 1

I bear that you gave to me. You, you, you ought - a know.

Gtr. 3

Gtr. 2

Gtr. 4

Gtr. 2 *divisi*

full

* Gtr. 4 to left in TAB.

Guitar Notation Legend

Guitar Music can be notated three different ways: on a *musical staff*, in *tablature*, and in *rhythm slashes*.

RHYTHM SLASHES are written above the staff. Strum chords in the rhythm indicated. Use the chord diagrams found at the top of the first page of the transcription for the appropriate chord voicings. Round noteheads indicate single notes.

THE MUSICAL STAFF shows pitches and rhythms and is divided by bar lines into measures. Pitches are named after the first seven letters of the alphabet.

TABLATURE graphically represents the guitar fingerboard. Each horizontal line represents a a string, and each number represents a fret.

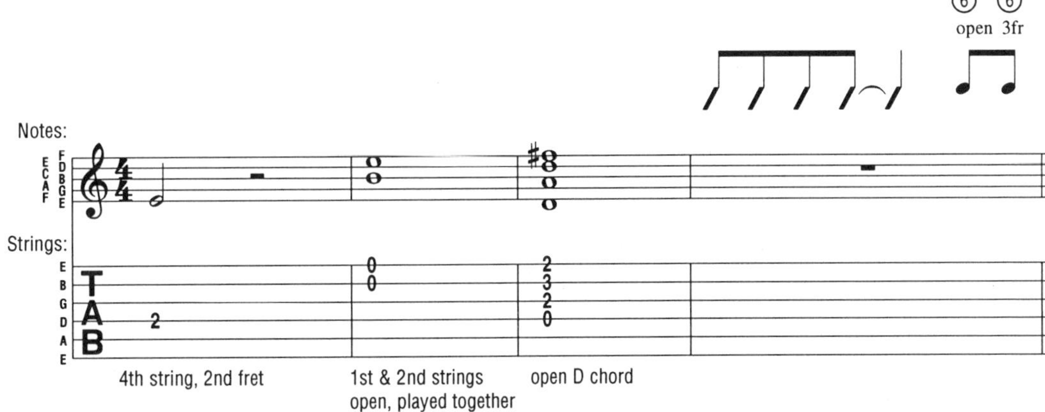

Definitions for Special Guitar Notation

HALF-STEP BEND: Strike the note and bend up 1/2 step.

WHOLE-STEP BEND: Strike the note and bend up one step.

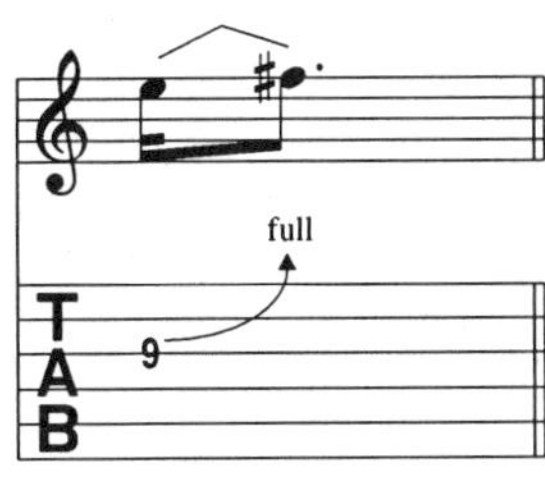

GRACE NOTE BEND: Strike the note and bend up as indicated. The first note does not take up any time.

SLIGHT (MICROTONE) BEND: Strike the note and bend up 1/4 step.

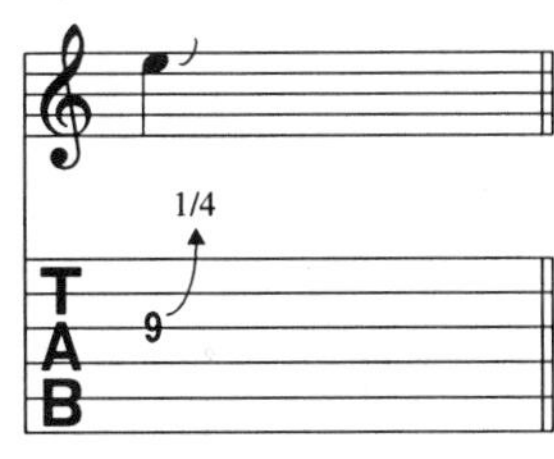

BEND AND RELEASE: Strike the note and bend up as indicated, then release back to the original note. Only the first note is struck.

PRE-BEND: Bend the note as indicated, then strike it.

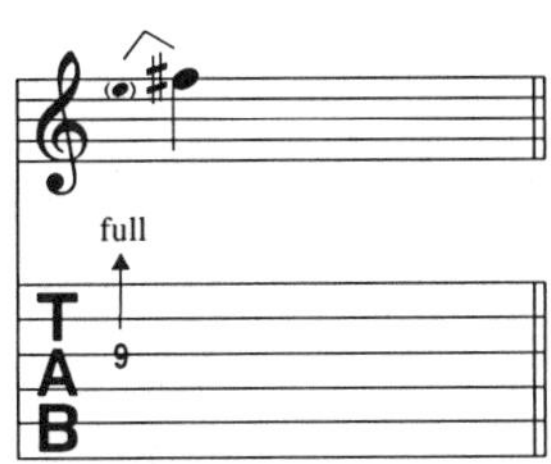

PRE-BEND AND RELEASE: Bend the note as indicated. Strike it and release the bend back to the original note.

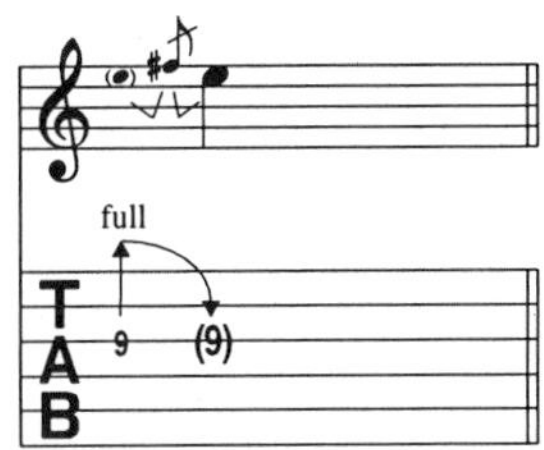

UNISON BEND: Strike the two notes simultaneously and bend the lower note up to the pitch of the higher.

VIBRATO: The string is vibrated by rapidly bending and releasing the note with the fretting hand.

WIDE VIBRATO: The pitch is varied to a greater degree by vibrating with the fretting hand.

HAMMER-ON: Strike the first (lower) note with one finger, then sound the higher note (on the same string) with another finger by fretting it without picking.

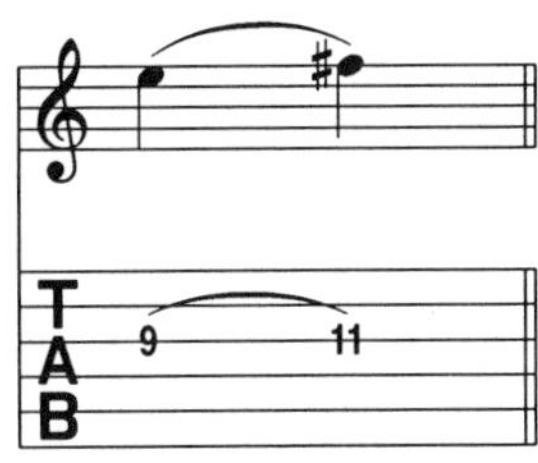

PULL-OFF: Place both fingers on the notes to be sounded. Strike the first note and without picking, pull the finger off to sound the second (lower) note.

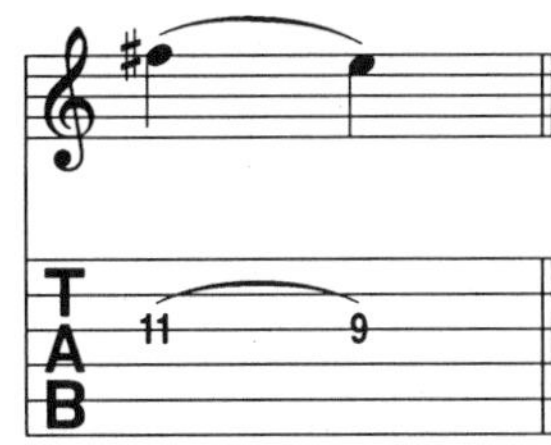

LEGATO SLIDE: Strike the first note and then slide the same fret-hand finger up or down to the second note. The second note is not struck.

SHIFT SLIDE: Same as legato slide, except the second note is struck.

TRILL: Very rapidly alternate between the notes indicated by continuously hammering on and pulling off.

TAPPING: Hammer ("tap") the fret indicated with the pick-hand index or middle finger and pull off to the note fretted by the fret hand.

NATURAL HARMONIC: Strike the note while the fret-hand lightly touches the string directly over the fret indicated.

PINCH HARMONIC: The note is fretted normally and a harmonic is produced by adding the edge of the thumb or the tip of the index finger of the pick hand to the normal pick attack.

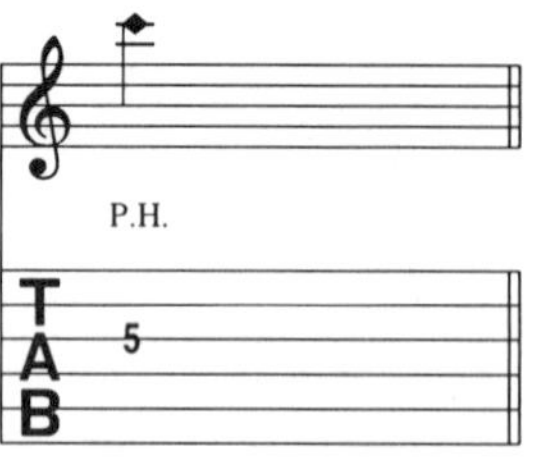

HARP HARMONIC: The note is fretted normally and a harmonic is produced by gently resting the pick hand's index finger directly above the indicated fret (in parentheses) while the pick hand's thumb or pick assists by plucking the appropriate string.

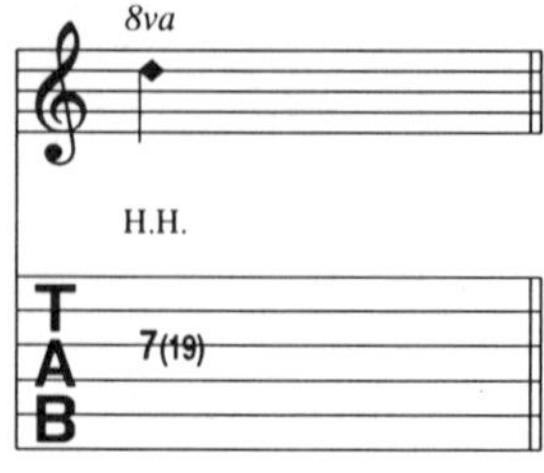

PICK SCRAPE: The edge of the pick is rubbed down (or up) the string, producing a scratchy sound.

MUFFLED STRINGS: A percussive sound is produced by laying the fret hand across the string(s) without depressing, and striking them with the pick hand.

PALM MUTING: The note is partially muted by the pick hand lightly touching the string(s) just before the bridge.

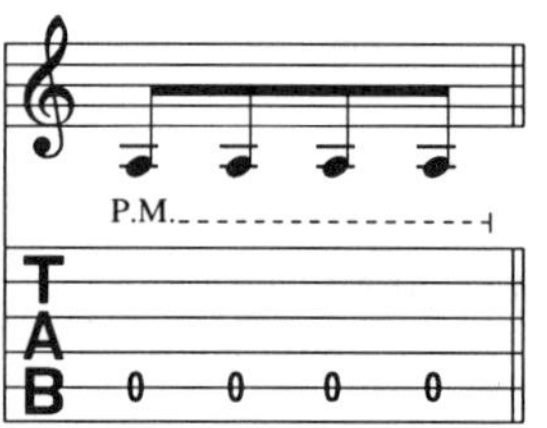

RAKE: Drag the pick across the strings indicated with a single motion.

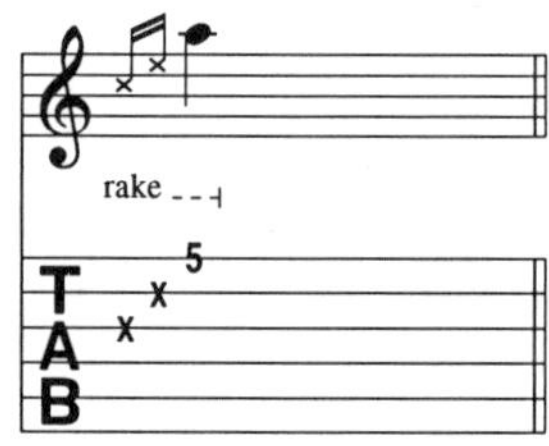

TREMOLO PICKING: The note is picked as rapidly and continuously as possible.

ARPEGGIATE: Play the notes of the chord indicated by quickly rolling them from bottom to top.

VIBRATO BAR DIVE AND RETURN: The pitch of the note or chord is dropped a specified number of steps (in rhythm) then returned to the original pitch.

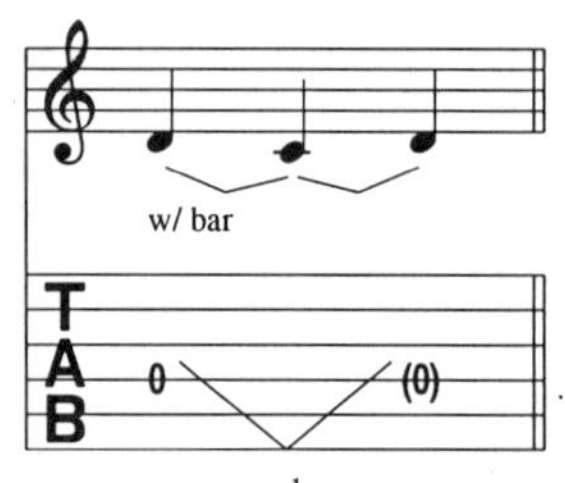

VIBRATO BAR SCOOP: Depress the bar just before striking the note, then quickly release the bar.

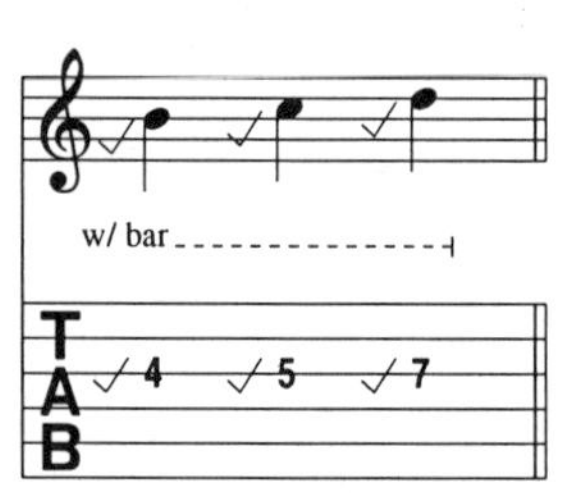

VIBRATO BAR DIP: Strike the note and then immediately drop a specified number of steps, then release back to the original pitch.

-1/2 -1/2 -1/2

w/ bar

-1/2 -1/2 -1/2

7 7 7

Additional Musical Definitions

(accent)	• Accentuate note (play it louder)	
(accent)	• Accentuate note with great intensity	
(staccato)	• Play the note short	
⊓	• Downstroke	
V	• Upstroke	
D.S. al Coda	• Go back to the sign (𝄋), then play until the measure marked "***To Coda,***" then skip to the section labelled "***Coda.***"	
D.S. al Fine	• Go back to the beginning of the song and play until the measure marked "***Fine***" (end).	

Rhy. Fig.	• Label used to recall a recurring accompaniment pattern (usually chordal).
Riff	• Label used to recall composed, melodic lines (usually single notes) which recur.
Fill	• Label used to identify a brief melodic figure which is to be inserted into the arrangement.
Rhy. Fill	• A chordal version of a Fill.
tacet	• Instrument is silent (drops out).
	• Repeat measures between signs.
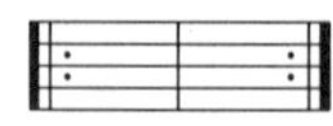	• When a repeated section has different endings, play the first ending only the first time and the second ending only the second time.

NOTE: Tablature numbers in parentheses mean:
1. The note is being sustained over a system (note in standard notation is tied), or
2. The note is sustained, but a new articulation (such as a hammer-on, pull-off, slide or vibrato begins, or
3. The note is a barely audible "ghost" note (note in standard notation is also in parentheses).

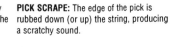

RECORDED VERSIONS

The Best Note-For-Note Transcriptions Available

RECORDED VERSIONS GUITAR

ALL BOOKS INCLUDE TABLATURE

00690199 Aerosmith – Nine Lives $19.95
00690146 Aerosmith – Toys in the Attic $19.95
00694865 Alice In Chains – Dirt $19.95
00694932 Allman Brothers Band – Volume 1 .... $24.95
00694933 Allman Brothers Band – Volume 2 .... $24.95
00694934 Allman Brothers Band – Volume 3 .... $24.95
00694877 Chet Atkins – Guitars For All Seasons $19.95
00694918 Randy Bachman Collection $22.95
00694880 Beatles – Abbey Road $19.95
00694863 Beatles – Sgt. Pepper's Lonely Hearts Club Band $19.95
00690174 Beck – Mellow Gold $17.95
00690346 Beck – Mutations $19.95
00690175 Beck – Odelay $17.95
00694884 The Best of George Benson $19.95
00692385 Chuck Berry $19.95
00692200 Black Sabbath – We Sold Our Soul For Rock 'N' Roll $19.95
00690115 Blind Melon – Soup $19.95
00690305 Blink 182 – Dude Ranch $19.95
00690241 Bloodhound Gang – One Fierce Beer Coaster $19.95
00690028 Blue Oyster Cult – Cult Classics $19.95
00690219 Blur $19.95
00694935 Boston: Double Shot Of $22.95
00690237 Meredith Brooks – Blurring the Edges $19.95
00690168 Roy Buchanon Collection $19.95
00690337 Jerry Cantrell – Boggy Depot $19.95
00690293 Best of Steven Curtis Chapman $19.95
00690043 Cheap Trick – Best Of $19.95
00120151 Best of the Chemical Brothers $14.95
00690171 Chicago – Definitive Guitar Collection $22.95
00660139 Eric Clapton – Journeyman $19.95
00694869 Eric Clapton – Live Acoustic $19.95
00694896 John Mayall/Eric Clapton – Bluesbreakers $19.95
00690162 Best of the Clash $19.95
00690166 Albert Collins – The Alligator Years $16.95
00694940 Counting Crows – August & Everything After $19.95
00690197 Counting Crows – Recovering the Satellites $19.95
00690118 Cranberries – The Best of $19.95
00690215 Music of Robert Cray $19.95
00694840 Cream – Disraeli Gears $19.95
00690007 Danzig 4 .... $19.95
00690184 DC Talk – Jesus Freak $19.95
00660186 Alex De Grassi Guitar Collection $19.95
00690289 Best of Deep Purple $17.95
00694831 Derek And The Dominos – Layla & Other Assorted Love Songs $19.95
00690322 Ani Di Franco – Little Plastic Castle $19.95
00690187 Dire Straits – Brothers In Arms $19.95
00690191 Dire Straits – Money For Nothing $24.95
00660178 Willie Dixon – Master Blues Composer $24.95
00690250 Best of Duane Eddy $16.95
00690323 Fastball – All the Pain Money Can Buy $19.95
00690089 Foo Fighters $19.95
00690235 Foo Fighters – The Colour and the Shape $19.95
00690042 Robben Ford Blues Collection $19.95
00694920 Free – Best Of $18.95
00690324 Fuel – Sunburn $19.95
00690222 G3 Live – Satriani, Vai, Johnson $22.95
00694894 Frank Gambale – The Great Explorers $19.95
00694807 Danny Gatton – 88 Elmira St $19.95
00690127 Goo Goo Dolls – A Boy Named Goo $19.95
00690338 Goo Goo Dolls – Dizzy Up the Girl $19.95
00690117 John Gorka Collection $19.95
00690114 Buddy Guy Collection Vol. A-J $22.95
00690193 Buddy Guy Collection Vol. L-Y $22.95
00694798 George Harrison Anthology $19.95

00690068 Return Of The Hellecasters $19.95
00692930 Jimi Hendrix – Are You Experienced? $24.95
00692931 Jimi Hendrix – Axis: Bold As Love $22.95
00692932 Jimi Hendrix – Electric Ladyland $24.95
00690218 Jimi Hendrix – First Rays of the New Rising Sun $24.95
00690038 Gary Hoey – Best Of $19.95
00660029 Buddy Holly $19.95
00660169 John Lee Hooker – A Blues Legend $19.95
00690054 Hootie & The Blowfish – Cracked Rear View $19.95
00694905 Howlin' Wolf $19.95
00690136 Indigo Girls – 1200 Curfews $22.95
00694938 Elmore James – Master Electric Slide Guitar $19.95
00690167 Skip James Blues Guitar Collection $16.95
00694833 Billy Joel For Guitar $19.95
00694912 Eric Johnson – Ah Via Musicom $19.95
00690169 Eric Johnson – Venus Isle $22.95
00694799 Robert Johnson – At The Crossroads $19.95
00693185 Judas Priest – Vintage Hits $19.95
00690277 Best of Kansas $19.95
00690073 B. B. King – 1950-1957 .... $24.95
00690098 B. B. King – 1958-1967 .... $24.95
00690099 B. B. King – 1962-1971 .... $24.95
00690134 Freddie King Collection $17.95
00694903 The Best Of Kiss $24.95
00690157 Kiss – Alive $19.95
00690163 Mark Knopfler/Chet Atkins – Neck and Neck $19.95
00690296 Patty Larkin Songbook $17.95
00690202 Live – Secret Samadhi $19.95
00690070 Live – Throwing Copper $19.95
00690018 Living Colour – Best Of $19.95
00694954 Lynyrd Skynyrd, New Best Of $19.95
00694845 Yngwie Malmsteen – Fire And Ice $19.95
00694956 Bob Marley – Legend $19.95
00690283 Best of Sarah McLachlan $19.95
00690239 Matchbox 20 – Yourself or Someone Like You $19.95
00690244 Megadeath – Cryptic Writings $19.95
00690236 Mighty Mighty Bosstones – Let's Face It $19.95
00690040 Steve Miller Band Greatest Hits $19.95
00690225 Moist – Creature $19.95
00694802 Gary Moore – Still Got The Blues $19.95
00690103 Alanis Morissette – Jagged Little Pill $19.95
00690341 Alanis Morisette – Supposed Former Infatuation Junkie $19.95
00694958 Mountain, Best Of $19.95
00694913 Nirvana – In Utero $19.95
00694883 Nirvana – Nevermind $19.95
00690026 Nirvana – Acoustic In New York $19.95
00120112 No Doubt – Tragic Kingdom $22.95
00690121 Oasis – (What's The Story) Morning Glory $19.95
00690290 Offspring, The – Ignition $19.95
00690204 Offspring, The – Ixnay on the Hombre $17.95
00690203 Offspring, The – Smash $17.95
00694830 Ozzy Osbourne – No More Tears $19.95
00694855 Pearl Jam – Ten $19.95
00690053 Liz Phair – Whip Smart $19.95
00690176 Phish – Billy Breathes $22.95
00690331 Phish – The Story of Ghost $19.95
00693800 Pink Floyd – Early Classics $19.95
00694967 Police – Message In A Box Boxed Set $70.00
00690195 Presidents of the United States of America II $22.95
00694974 Queen – A Night At The Opera $19.95
00690145 Rage Against The Machine – Evil Empire $19.95
00690179 Rancid – And Out Come the Wolves $22.95
00690055 Red Hot Chili Peppers – Bloodsugarsexmagik $19.95

00690090 Red Hot Chili Peppers – One Hot Minute $22.95
00694892 Guitar Style Of Jerry Reed $19.95
00694937 Jimmy Reed – Master Bluesman $19.95
00694899 R.E.M. – Automatic For The People $19.95
00690260 Jimmie Rodgers Guitar Collection $17.95
00690014 Rolling Stones – Exile On Main Street $24.95
00690186 Rolling Stones – Rock & Roll Circus $19.95
00690135 Otis Rush Collection $19.95
00690031 Santana's Greatest Hits $19.95
00694805 Scorpions – Crazy World $19.95
00690150 Son Seals – Bad Axe Blues $17.95
00690128 Seven Mary Three – American Standards $19.95
00690076 Sex Pistols – Never Mind The Bollocks $19.95
00120105 Kenny Wayne Shepherd – Ledbetter Heights $19.95
00120123 Kenny Wayne Shepherd – Trouble Is $19.95
00690196 Silverchair – Freak Show $19.95
00690130 Silverchair – Frogstomp $19.95
00690041 Smithereens – Best Of $19.95
00694885 Spin Doctors – Pocket Full Of Kryptonite $19.95
00690124 Sponge – Rotting Pinata $19.95
00120004 Steely Dan – Best Of $24.95
00694921 Steppenwolf, The Best Of $22.95
00694957 Rod Stewart – Acoustic Live $22.95
00690021 Sting – Fields Of Gold $19.95
00120081 Sublime $19.95
00120122 Sublime – 40 Oz. to Freedom $19.95
00690242 Suede – Coming Up $19.95
00694824 Best Of James Taylor $16.95
00694887 Thin Lizzy – The Best Of Thin Lizzy $19.95
00690238 Third Eye Blind $19.95
00690022 Richard Thompson Guitar $19.95
00690267 311 .... $19.95
00690030 Toad The Wet Sprocket $19.95
00690228 Tonic – Lemon Parade $19.95
00690295 Tool – Aenima $19.95
00694411 U2 – The Joshua Tree $19.95
00690039 Steve Vai – Alien Love Secrets $24.95
00690172 Steve Vai – Fire Garden $24.95
00690023 Jimmie Vaughan – Strange Pleasures $19.95
00660136 Stevie Ray Vaughan – In Step $19.95
00694835 Stevie Ray Vaughan – The Sky Is Crying $19.95
00694776 Vaughan Brothers – Family Style $19.95
00690217 Verve Pipe, The – Villains $19.95
00120026 Joe Walsh – Look What I Did... .... $24.95
00694789 Muddy Waters – Deep Blues $24.95
00690071 Weezer $19.95
00690286 Weezer – Pinkerton $19.95
00694970 Who, The – Definitive Collection A-E $24.95
00694971 Who, The – Definitive Collection F-Li $24.95
00694972 Who, The – Definitive Collection Lo-R $24.95
00694973 Who, The – Definitive Collection S-Y $24.95
00690320 Best of Dar Williams $17.95
00690319 Best of Stevie Wonder $19.95

All books include standard notation and guitar tablature.

THE BEST

ROCK GUITAR COLLECTIONS

FOR MORE INFORMATION,
SEE YOUR LOCAL MUSIC DEALER,
OR WRITE TO:

HAL•LEONARD®
CORPORATION
7777 W. BLUEMOUND RD. P.O. BOX 13819
MILWAUKEE, WISCONSIN 53213

RECORDED VERSIONS GUITAR
AUTHENTIC TRANSCRIPTIONS WITH NOTES AND TABLATURE

'60s GUITAR CLASSICS

25 classic hits, including: All Day and All of the Night • Born to Be Wild • Brown Eyed Girl • Evil Ways • Hey Joe • Secret Agent Man • The Sunshine of Your Love • Turn! Turn! Turn! • Wild Thing • and more.
00690206 Guitar Recorded Versions $15.95

'70s GUITAR CLASSICS

25 must-know songs for guitarists, including: All Right Now • The Boys Are Back in Town • Changes • Detroit Rock City • Don't Fear the Reaper • Free Ride • Heartache Tonight • Iron Man • Layla • Message in a Bottle • Money • Sultans of Swing • Walk This Way • and more.
00690207 Guitar Recorded Versions $17.95

'80s GUITAR CLASSICS

25 hits from the 1980s for guitar, including: Addicted to Love • Brass in Pocket • Crazy Train • Every Breath You Take • Money for Nothing • Owner of a Lonely Heart • Pride and Joy • Should I Stay or Should I Go • Sweet Child O' Mine • You Give Love a Bad Name • and more.
00690208 Guitar Recorded Versions $15.95

ACOUSTIC GUITAR CLASSICS

12 songs, including: And I Love Her • Angie • Dee • Dust in the Wind • Greensleeves • Layla • The Magic Bus • Melissa • More Than a Feeling • Norwegian Wood (This Bird Has Flown) • Patience • You've Got a Friend.
00690151 Guitar Recorded Versions $14.95

ACOUSTIC ROCK IN THE 90S

12 hits, including: All I Want • Here and Now • The Man Who Sold the World • My Friends • Name • Only Wanna Be with You • Tears in Heaven • Wonderwall • and more.
00690155 Guitar Recorded Versions $14.95

ALTERNATIVE ROCK COLLECTION

16 songs, including: Backwater • Black Hole Sun • Buddy Holly • Come As You Are • Girlfriend • Hold My Hand • Losing My Religion • Supernova • What's the Frequency, Kenneth? • Zombie • and more.
00690060 Guitar Recorded Versions $19.95

BEST OF CONTEMPORARY ROCK

Book/CD Pack

This book/CD pack includes complete note-for-note transcriptions plus a CD with 48 tracks including half-speed demonstrations, effects settings, performance notes and more. Includes: All for You • Barely Breathing • Come Down • The Distance • Lovefool • Santeria • Spiderwebs • Where It's At • Where You Get Love • You Were Meant for Me.
00690220 Guitar Recorded Versions $17.95

BEST OF MODERN ROCK

Book/CD Pack

This book/CD pack includes complete note-for-note guitar transcriptions plus a CD with 44 tracks, including isolated guitar parts and reduced speed demonstrations. 9 contemporary favorites: Freak • If You Could Only See • The Impression That I Get • Semi-Charmed Life • Song 2 • more.
00690221 Guitar Recorded Versions $17.95

BRITISH INVASION GUITAR CLASSICS

14 classics, including: All Day and All of the Night • For Your Love • I Can See for Miles • My Generation • Not Fade Away • Sunshine of Your Love • We Gotta Get Out of This Place • and more.
00690213 Guitar Recorded Versions $14.95

CLASSIC ROCK INSTRUMENTALS

Transcribed by Fred Sokolow

A big collection of 29 songs that have become classics because of their guitar riffs, including: (Ghost) Riders in the Sky • Hawaii Five-O • Pipeline • Scuttle Buttin' • Sleepwalk • Wipe Out • and more.
00694793 Guitar Recorded Versions $18.95

CONTEMPORARY ROCK HITS

10 complete transcriptions for guitar, including: Change the World • Counting Blue Cars • Crash Into Me • Free • You Learn • and more.
00690201 Guitar Recorded Versions $12.95

FOLK-ROCK GUITAR COLLECTION

14 folk-rock favorites, including: American Pie • At Seventeen • Fire and Rain • Leaving on a Jet Plane • Southern Cross • Take Me Home, Country Roads • Taxi • Turn! Turn! Turn! • You're So Vain • and more.
00690205 Guitar Recorded Versions $16.95

FUNK GUITAR COLLECTION

17 songs, including: Apache Rose Peacock • Big Fat Funky Booty • But It's Alright • Free Ride • Funk #49 • It's Your Thing • Love Rears Its Ugly Head • Shining Star • and more.
00690101 Guitar Recorded Versions $19.95

GENUINE ROCKABILLY GUITAR HITS

Over 20 classics, including: American Music • Everybody's Tryin' to Be My Baby • My Baby Thinks He's a Train • Rock Around the Clock • Rock This Town • Summertime Blues • Tear It Up • and more.
00694848 Guitar Recorded Versions $19.95

GREATEST ROCK STANDARDS

22 songs every rock guitarist should know, including: All Right Now • Born to Be Wild • My Generation • Rock and Roll All Nite • Takin' Care of Business • Wild Thing • You Really Got Me • and more.
00690254 Guitar Recorded Versions $14.95

Prices, contents, and availability subject to change without notice. Some products may not be available outside the U.S.A.